# Simple PASCAL

# Simple PASCAL

James J McGregor
*and* Alan H Watt

Department of Computer Science
University of Sheffield

PITMAN PUBLISHING
128 Long Acre, London WC 2E 9AN

A Division of Longman Group UK Limited

First published in Great Britain 1981
Reprinted 1982, 1983, 1984, 1985, 1986, 1987, 1988, 1989, 1990, 1991

Produced by Longman Group (FE) Ltd
Printed in Hong Kong

ISBN 0 273 01704 7

# Preface

A computer program is a set of instructions which tell a computer how to carry out a calculation or perform some other operation. These instructions have to be expressed in one of the many computer programming languages available. PASCAL is one such language which is currently becoming very widely used.

The purpose of this book is to teach you how to write computer programs in PASCAL. It is intended to be a genuine introductory text for beginners. The main problem encountered by beginners is in expressing what they want the computer to do in terms of the instructions available in the programming language being used. For this reason, we aim at teaching how to write programs in PASCAL without presenting more information than is absolutely necessary about the internal operation of the computer. Unnecessary use of computing jargon is also avoided.

We do not attempt to cover the complete PASCAL language, but concentrate on a central part that is adequate for writing a wide range of useful programs. The material covered will be sufficient for the needs of the casual programmer who needs occasionally to use the computer for solving problems. A mastery of the material in this book will also provide a solid foundation on which to base further study of advanced programming techniques and of computer science generally.

Throughout the book, general ideas are introduced by means of examples. At first, the examples are extremely simple programs that may not seem convincingly useful. We must ask the reader to be very patient: a clear understanding of the elementary techniques introduced in these examples is essential before programs of real practical use can be written. We believe that programming is a skill learned mainly by reading and writing programs, and we urge the reader to attempt most of the exercises set at the end of each chapter.

This book is written in two languages: English and PASCAL. To distinguish between them, PASCAL text is framed in boxes.

# Contents

# Introduction

The following very simple PASCAL program will be used to illustrate a number of fundamental points. We shall explain shortly what this program tells the computer to do.

```
program room(output);

begin
    writeln('your room needs ', 3*2, ' sq.m. of vinyl');
    writeln('and ', 2*(3+2)*3, ' sq.m. of wallcovering.')
end.
```

Notice that some of the words in the program are underlined. Words like these have a special meaning in PASCAL programs. Underlining them makes them stand out and makes a printed or handwritten program easier to read.

Unless it has special equipment, a computer cannot read characters that are simply typed on paper. A common way of getting a program into a computer is to type it on a typewriter keyboard that is somehow connected to the computer. Another way is to type it on special apparatus that punches a different pattern of holes corresponding to each different character. These holes are punched in cards in a manner that allows the computer to read a program easily. When you find out how to get programs into your particular computer you may find that only capital letters are available, and programs may have to be typed (without underlining) as follows:

```
PROGRAM ROOM(OUTPUT);

BEGIN
    WRITELN('YOUR ROOM NEEDS ', 3*2, ' SQ.M. OF VINYL');
    WRITELN('AND ', 2*(3+2)*3, ' SQ.M. OF WALLCOVERING.')
END.
```

Once a program has been typed into the computer, the computer can attempt to obey it. This may happen automatically on the computer you are using, or you may have to type a command at the keyboard telling the computer to obey the program. This process of obeying the program is often referred to as **execution** of the program.

The first line of our introductory program:

```
program room(output);
```

contains the name - "room" - that we have invented for this particular program. The word "output" in brackets tells the computer to be ready to print something when the program is obeyed. The part of the program which tells the computer what to do comes between begin and end. Here we always have a list of statements (only two in this case) separated by semicolons. In PASCAL, a so-called statement is in fact an instruction which tells the computer to do something. The first statement obeyed in this program is

```
writeln('your room needs ', 3*2, ' sq.m. of vinyl')
```

This tells the computer to print the information specified between the brackets. In this case we have three items, separated from each other by commas, to be printed:

| | |
|---|---|
| 'your room needs ' | The characters between the quotation marks are printed exactly as they stand. |
| 3*2 | The value of the expression is calculated and printed. (We use * as a multiplication sign.) |
| ' sq.m. of vinyl' | The characters between the quotation marks are printed exactly as they stand. |

Thus when the computer obeys this statement it will print:

your room needs 6 sq.m. of vinyl

Depending on the computer system you are using, the output may be typed on paper at your keyboard, it may appear on a video screen attached to your keyboard, or it may be printed on a device known as a line-printer. The exact layout used for printing the numerical value 6 will vary from one PASCAL system to another. Your system may print extra spaces before the number.

The appearance of the characters "ln" at the end of the word "writeln" indicates that subsequent output is to be produced at the start of a new line. This is explained in more detail later.

When the computer has obeyed one statement it goes on to the next. Thus, when the computer obeys our introductory program, it will print the floor area and wall area of a 3m.x2m.x3m. room:

your room needs 6 sq.m. of vinyl
and 30 sq.m. of wallcovering.

In order to make it easy for a program to be processed by a machine, the grammatical rules in PASCAL are very strict. You will find, for example, that you must put commas and semicolons in just the right places. If you do not, the computer will report that there is a **syntax error** in your program and will not be able to obey it. The rules for the layout of a program are less strict. We can insert as many spaces as we like between the words, symbols and numbers in the program, providing that we insert at least one space between words. We are also free to choose how we set the program out on separate lines, as long as we do not start a new line in the middle of a word or number. We shall make use of this freedom of layout to make our programs as readable as possible. This is very important, not only because we may wish someone else to read and understand our programs, but also because we may wish to re-read them ourselves at some later date when we want to extend or modify them.

Even if a program is grammatically or syntactically correct, and the computer attempts to obey it, something may go wrong while the program is being obeyed. For example, the result of a calculation may be a number that is too big for your computer to handle. If such an **execution error** occurs, the computer will stop obeying your program and print out a message explaining what has happened.

You should remember that, even if the computer successfully executes a program, this does not necessarily mean that correct answers have been produced. If, in our introductory program, we mistyped the expression for the wall area as "2*(3-2)*3", telling the computer to subtract the length of our room from its width, the computer would still successfully obey the program. It would print

your room needs 6 sq.m. of vinyl
and 6 sq.m. of wallcovering.

which is of course wrong.

Programs, once written, can be obeyed over and over again and this is one of the main advantages of a computer. We could, for instance, write a weekly payroll program which is executed 52 times a year. Our introductory example is not very useful however, because if it were obeyed again it would produce exactly the same output.

Programs are usually written in more general terms so that the calculations described in a program can be performed on different numbers or **data** on different occasions. For example, a payroll program would have to be given the number of hours worked by each employee during the current week, current rates of pay, and so on.

Our "room" program calculates the floor and wall areas for a room with particular dimensions. A program which could perform the same calculations, but for different rooms on different occasions, would be more generally useful. Making a program general in this sense is one of the main topics in Chapter 1.

# 1 Getting information in and out

In this chapter, we describe various ways of getting information into and out of the computer while a program is being obeyed. The material in Sections 1.5 and 1.6 is best presented as part of this chapter, but these sections could be omitted on a first reading.

## 1.1 Getting information into a program

The PASCAL statement

```
writeln('your room needs ', 3*2, ' sq.m. of vinyl')
```

causes the computer to write or print three things:

1) the text 'your room needs ',
2) the value of the expression 3*2 which is 6,
3) the text ' sq.m. of vinyl'.

When this statement is obeyed, the computer prints:

your room needs 6 sq.m. of vinyl

In order to make our introductory program more flexible, we consider

```
writeln('your room needs ', length*width,
        ' sq.m. of vinyl')
```

in which we have replaced a particular expression, "3*2", by a more general one: "length*width". In the program, "length" and "width" are going to be the names of two variables. We can think of a variable as a named box in which a program can store something:

length    | 3 |        width    | 2 |

We can say that "length" is the name of a box containing 3 and "width" is the name of a box containing 2. We shall soon see how these values get there. When the computer evaluates the expression "length*width" it multiplies the **contents** of "length" by the

**contents** of "width". Of course the boxes "length" and "width" need not necessarily contain the numbers 3 and 2. They could contain any numbers that are not too big for the size of the box (more about that later).

For example:

length ┌──────┐ 50 └──────┘    width ┌──────┐ 35 └──────┘

This is why we use the term **variable**.   Now we can rewrite our program "room" in such a way that each time it is executed or obeyed different numbers may be put in the boxes "length" and "width".


Program 1.1
This program works out the amount of floor and wall covering required for a room of **any** length, width and height.

```
program roomsize(input,output);

var length, width, height : integer;

begin

    read(length, width, height);
    writeln('your room needs ', length*width,
            ' sq.m. of vinyl');
    writeln('and ', 2*(length + width)*height,
            ' sq.m. of wallcovering')
end.
```

The second line of the program simply tells the computer to set aside space for three variables, "length", "width" and "height". More information about this appears in Section 1.3.

The statement:

```
read(length, width, height)
```

is the means whereby particular values are put in boxes "length", "width" and "height" each time the program is executed. When the computer obeys this statement it pauses and waits until 3 numbers are supplied. We shall assume, for the time being, that such numbers are supplied directly from a keyboard while the computer is obeying the program:

5

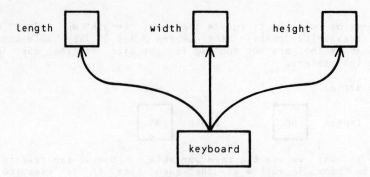

The program then continues execution and evaluates the general expressions

    length*width

and

    2*(length + width)*height

using the values for "length", "width" and "height" which are contained in the boxes with these names. These are the values which have just been supplied from the keyboard. The appearance of the word "input" in the first line of the above program tells the computer to be prepared to receive input during the execution of the program. The values supplied as input are sometimes called the **data** for the program. When numbers are typed as input for a PASCAL program, they are separated by spaces (as many as we like) and can be spread over as many lines as we like.

## 1.2 Executing a program

    After you have typed your program it is stored in a way peculiar to your own computer. You have given your program a name in the first line – let us assume that your system uses this name to distinguish it from other programs that you may have written and stored.     To make the computer obey or execute your program you have to type something like:

    execute roomsize

where "execute" is the command which causes the computer to execute your program. This is not a PASCAL statement but a command which tells the computer what to do with a PASCAL program. The commands for your computer are probably different. The result of executing the program could be a display like:

    ? execute roomsize
    ? 3    2    3
    your room needs 6 sq.m. of vinyl
    and 30 sq.m. of wallcovering

The two lines preceded by a question mark are lines typed by the person using the program. When a computer expects you to type a

6

command or numbers from the keyboard, it will print some sort of "invitation to type", usually called a prompt. Whether this prompt is a question mark, a phrase like "what next" or something else will again depend on your particular system. Thus in the above illustration the information following the question marks is typed by the user and the remainder by the computer. Program "roomsize" could be re-executed using diferent values. This might produce the following:

```
? execute roomsize
? 5    3    3
your room needs 15 sq.m. of vinyl
and 48 sq.m. of wallcovering
```

Now when a program is to be controlled from a keyboard as above, it is good programming practice to precede a read statement with a write statement which prints a message telling or reminding the user what to type next. If we execute a particular program months after it has been written, or if another person (not the programmer) executes the program, then it is vital that the program informs the user what information is to be typed and in what order.

## Program 1.2

This is identical to program 1.1 except that the program will type a request for input when it is required.

```
program roomsize2(input,output);

var length, width, height : integer;

begin

    writeln('type in length, width and height');
    read(length, width, height);

    writeln('your room needs ', length*width,
            ' sq.m. of vinyl');
    writeln('and ', 2*(length + width)*height,
            ' sq.m. of wall covering')
end.
```

This will produce a display like the following:

```
? execute roomsize2
type in length, width and height
? 3    2    4
your room needs 6 sq.m. of vinyl
and 40 sq.m. of wall covering
```

The appearance of the second line in the display serves to remind you or another user, what the program does and the information it requires. We will not always do this in examples in this book because it adds nothing to the instructive value of the program; but you should always use the technique in practice.

One further point that you should bear in mind when operating a computer from a keyboard is that, when you are requested to type something, the computer may be in one of several states. For example, it may be waiting for you to type the next line of a PASCAL program; it may be waiting for a command telling it to execute a program or to modify it in some way; it may be waiting for data to be typed into a program that is currently being executed. The computer must always be provided with the kind of information it expects.

## 1.3 Variables and declarations

In programs 1.1 and 1.2 the line:

```
var length, width, height : integer;
```

gives the computer three pieces of information: you require three boxes or variables; the names of these boxes are to be "length", "width" and "height"; you are going to put quantities in these boxes which are integer numbers or whole numbers. This is called a variable declaration and in its simplest form comprises two parts:

1) A list of names chosen by the programmer, and separated by commas. A name consists of a sequence of letters and numeric digits starting with a letter; except that reserved words like "begin" , "end", "var" etc. must not be used. The words are of course reserved just so that there is no confusion between these words and variable names. A complete list of reserved words is given in Appendix 1. At this stage, you do not need to know what all the reserved words mean but you must not attempt to use them as variable names.
   You should choose mnemonically meaningful names. For example in the above context choose the names "length", "width" and "height" rather than "l", "w" and "h", or worse still "x", "y" and "z". This makes it much easier for your program to be read by other people or by yourself in the future if you wish to develop it further. Names can be of any length but you may find your particular computer system specifies a maximum length. Spaces must not be typed in the middle of a word; but this is not too inconvenient, it means you must use, for example, "nooftimes" rather than "no of times".

2) The type of quantity the box is going to contain. For the moment we are going to use only two types : "integer" and "real". A real number is a number with a fractional part.
   Real numbers and integers are represented in different ways inside the computer and there are good reasons for distinguishing between them in a program. You need not worry about the reasons for the distinction. You only need to

8

remember that the computer will not allow you to put a real number into an integer variable. (It will, however, allow you to put an integer value into a real variable.) Integer variables are generally used in a program for counting things and real variables are used for holding the results of arithmetic calculations.

Now consider the following examples:

```
var noofyears, noofmonths : integer;
```

means that the program is going to use two variables called "noofyears" and "noofmonths" which are going to contain integers, for example:

noofyears  53        noofmonths  4

The following declaration:

```
var temperature : real;
```

means that the program is going to use one variable called "temperature" which is going to contain a real number, for example:

temperature  93.75

The following declaration:

```
var noofyears, noofmonths : integer;
    temperature : real;
```

means the program is going to use three variables two of which are going to contain integers and one a real number. Note that the word var appears only once in such a declaration.

Now there is a limit to the maximum size of integers which can be put in an integer variable and similarly a limit to the maximum size of real numbers which can be put in a real variable. These limits are dependent on your particular computer system and you will find them in the manufacturer's literature.

Incidentally, for reasons we can't go into at this stage, the words "real" and "integer" are not reserved words, but it would be inadvisable to try to use them as variable names.

Program 1.3
Calculates the outstanding debt on a loan after a monthly payment
has been made.

```
program loanrepayment(input,output);

var debt, monthlyrate, payment : real;

begin

    writeln('type in debt, monthly rate and payment');
    read(debt, monthlyrate, payment);
    write('debt after next payment is ');
    writeln(debt + debt*monthlyrate/100 - payment)

end.
```

You should note that this is a very simple program which does not
take into account the fact that the payment may be greater than
the outstanding debt. This possibility will be dealt with in
subsequent chapters. The difference between "write" and
"writeln" is explained in the next section.


## 1.4 Getting information out of a program - simple output

Up to now we have been using "write" and "writeln" in various
contexts where it seems reasonably obvious from the context what
the effect will be. We will now look in more detail at the
behaviour of such write-statements.

Consider the following examples:


| statement | computer prints |
|---|---|
| writeln(25) | 25 |
| writeln(3*2) | 6 |
| writeln('3 x 2 = ', 3*2) | 3 x 2 = 6 |


From these examples we can note three facts:

1) A write-statement includes, in round brackets, a list of
   entities to be printed. Entities in the list are separated by
   commas.

2) Any entity enclosed in single quotation marks is printed
   exactly as it is written in the program. The computer simply
   reproduces such entities which are called messages or strings.

3) For any entity not enclosed in single quotation marks the
   computer prints a value, possibly after doing a calculation to
   obtain this value.

Here are two more examples. We assume that "length" contains 5 and "width" contains 3.

length [5]     width [3]

| statement | computer prints |
|---|---|
| writeln(length*width) | 15 |
| writeln('area is ', length*width) | area is 15 |

An entity not enclosed in single quotation marks can be just a single variable name. For example if the variables "x" and "y" contain the numbers shown:

x [7]     y [2]

| statement | computer prints |
|---|---|
| writeln(x) | 7 |
| writeln(y) | 2 |
| writeln('x contains ',x) | x contains 7 |
| writeln('y contains ',y) | y contains 2 |
| writeln('sum of x & y is ',x+y) | sum of x & y is 9 |
| writeln('sum of ',x,'& ',y,'is ',x+y) | sum of 7 & 2 is 9 |
| writeln('x + y = ',x + y) | x + y = 9 |
| writeln(x,' + ',y,' = ',x +y) | 7 + 2 = 9 |

You should examine carefully the differences in the effects of the last four statements.

In the absence of formatting information (as discussed in the next section) any values in a write-statement will be printed in some standard way which has been defined by the people who designed your particular PASCAL system. We shall assume throughout this book that, when formatting information is not used, integer numbers and real numbers are printed without any additional spaces before or after, and that reals are printed with two digits after the decimal point. Thus we will assume that

```
writeln(2*3, ' and ', 65.734*2)
```

produces

6 and 131.47

This may not match the conventions used in your system. In the absence of formatting information, most systems print reals in what is called floating-point form, for example:

1.31468E02

This is the computer's way of saying "1.31468 with the decimal point moved two places to the right", which is 131.468. This notation is useful mainly for representing very large or very small numbers. It is rather a clumsy notation for beginners and you can avoid it, if necessary, by providing formatting information as described in the next section.

The difference between "write" and "writeln" is that "writeln" causes the computer to start a new line of output **after** the list of entities has been printed.

For example:

| statements | computer prints |
|---|---|
| write('1st line ');<br>write('still on 1st line') | 1st line still on 1st line |
| writeln('1st line');<br>write ('2nd line') | 1st line<br>2nd line |

Note the use of "write" followed by "writeln" in Program 1.3. "writeln" can be used on its own (i.e. with no brackets) and this causes the computer to start a new line for subsequent output. This does not necessarily imply that a blank line is printed. For example:

| statements | computer prints |
|---|---|
| write('1st line');<br>writeln;<br>writeln('2nd line') | 1st line<br>2nd line |
| writeln('1st line');<br>writeln;<br>writeln('3rd line') | 1st line<br><br>3rd line |

12

Program 1.4
This is a simple program producing the following display on the
print device

```
                    *
                 *     *
              *           *
           *                 *
        *                       *
     *          triangle           *
  *                                   *
*                                       *
* * * * * * * * * * * * * * * * * * * *
```

```
program triangle(output);

begin

   writeln('                    *');
   writeln('                 *     *');
   writeln('              *           *');
   writeln('           *                 *');
   writeln('        *                       *');
   writeln('     *          triangle           *');
   writeln('  *                                   *');
   writeln(' *                                      *');
   writeln('* * * * * * * * * * * * * * * * * * * *')

end.
```

Note that this is a program to which we do not supply any input
information. Thus the word input does not appear on the first
line. Note also that the program does not contain any variables.


Program 1.5
Prints an electricity bill which looks, for example, like this:

```
******************************
present meter reading    6015
previous meter reading   5899
units used               116
rate per unit            3.4p
standing charge          £1.14

the sum due is           £5.08
******************************
```

Present meter reading and previous meter reading are to be typed
into the program. Rate per unit and standing charge are fixed as
shown above. Units used and the sum due are to be calculated. We
will see in Chapter 4 how to take into account the fact that the
previous meter reading could be greater than the present meter
reading if the meter has gone through its maximum of 10000, say,
and reset to zero.

```
program electricitybill(input,output);

var present, previous : integer;

begin

    read(present, previous);

    writeln('*****************************');

    writeln('present meter reading    ', present);
    writeln('previous meter reading   ', previous);

    writeln('units used               ',
                          present - previous);
    writeln('rate per unit         3.4p');
    writeln('standing charge       £1.14');

    writeln;
    write  ('the sum due is        £');
    writeln( (present - previous)*3.4/100 + 1.14 );

    writeln('*****************************')
end.
```

We have made use of extra spaces in the strings in an attempt to
line up the column of numbers printed by the computer on the
right. You will find it difficult in this type of context to get
the precise layout you want without the use of the facilities
discussed in the next section.

We have again used round brackets in this program where their
meaning should be fairly obvious. The use of round brackets will
be fully explained in Chapter 2. Note that the symbol "/" means
"divided by".


## 1.5 Getting information out of a program - formatted output

We can supply more information about the layout we require for
the values output by write-statements. This is done by providing
formatting information alongside an item in a write-statement. For
example:

```
writeln(2*256:8)
```

when obeyed will print:

512

with 5 additional spaces inserted before the number. The value 512
requires only three character widths when printed, but in this
example we have instructed the computer to make the total number

of characters up to 8, if necessary, by inserting additional
spaces before the value printed. Each item in the write-list can
be followed by formatting information. Integers and strings can be
followed by a single value indicating the minimum number of
characters the computer should use for printing that item, extra
spaces being inserted if necessary to make up the specified total.
(If more than the specified number of characters is needed, then,
of course, no extra spaces are inserted.)

The formatting facility is very useful when output values are
being lined up in columns. For example, given a variable "n" which
contains 9256, the following:

```
writeln('i':4, 'i*n':6);
writeln;
writeln(1:4, n:6);
writeln(2:4, 2*n:6);
writeln(3:4, 3*n:6)
```

will print

```
i   i*n

1   9256
2  18512
3  27768
```

By using the same format value in successive writeln statements,
values on separate lines can be easily lined up into columns. As
another example of formatting, the following sequence of
statements could be used to produce exactly the same output as
Program 1.4.

```
writeln('*':17);
writeln('*':15, '*': 4);
writeln('*':13, '*': 8);
writeln('*':11, '*':12);
writeln('*': 9, '*':16);
writeln('*': 7, 'triangle':13, '*':7);
writeln('*': 5, '*':24);
writeln('*': 3, '*':28);
writeln('* * * * * * * * * * * * * * * *')
```

In the case of real values, two pieces of formatting
information can be provided. The first indicates the minimum
number of characters to be printed altogether, and the second
indicates the number of digits to be printed after the decimal
point.

Thus if a variable "x" contains 9.479 and "y" contains 3.141592

```
writeln(x:8:4, y:10:5, x+y:9:2)
```

will print

9.4790   3.14159   12.62

Note that the number of characters printed includes the decimal point and the minus sign if any.

One way of using formatting information in Program 1.5 would be as follows:

```
writeln('present meter reading ', present:7);
writeln('previous meter reading', previous:7);
writeln('units used            ', present-previous:7);
writeln('rate per unit         ', 3.4 :6:1, 'p');
writeln('standing charge      £', 1.14:7:2);
write  ('the sum due is       £');
writeln( (present-previous)*3.4/100 + 1.14 :7:2 )
```

Here we have simply lined up the closing quotation mark at the end of each message, whereas previously we were unable to do this.

## 1.6 Named constants

Named constants are boxes into which a value is put before a program is obeyed. This value remains unchanged during the execution of the program and cannot be altered.

Program 1.6
This program prints the area and circumference of a circle of given radius.

```
program areaofcircle(input,output);

const pi = 3.14159;
var radius : real;

begin

   read(radius);
   writeln('the cicumference is ', 2*pi*radius);
   writeln('the area is        ', pi*radius*radius)

end.
```

16

You can see from this that named constants are declared before variables and that the declaration takes the form of a name, equals sign and value.

Let us illustrate two of the main advantages of using constants in a program by rewriting Program 1.5

Program 1.7
Prints an electricity bill given present and previous meter readings.

```
program electricitybill2(input,output);

const unitrate = 3.4;
      standcharge = 1.14;
      asterisks = '******************************';

var present, previous : integer;

begin

    read(present,previous);
    writeln(asterisks);
    writeln('present meter reading ', present:7);
    writeln('previous meter reading', previous:7);
    writeln('units used         ',
                    present - previous :7);
    writeln('rate per unit      ',
                    unitrate :6:1, 'p');
    writeln('standing charge      £', standcharge:7:2);
    writeln('sum due is           £',
      (present-previous)*unitrate/100+standcharge:7:2);
    writeln(asterisks)

end.
```

In the the above program the two values, standing charge and unit rate, will be the same each time the program is obeyed, over a fairly long period. Firstly, giving names to these values makes the program more readable. Secondly, if at some future date electricity prices rise, we can change the values of standing charge and unit rate very easily. Only the constant declaration needs changing. Otherwise we would have to change the appropriate values wherever they had been written into the text of the program. In a more lengthy program, standing charge and unit rate may have occurred a large number of times.

Note that in the above program there are three named constants in use and that they are separately declared. Also note the use of the string constant "asterisks".

Finally, an expression can not be used to specify a value for a constant. We can **not** write a constant declaration such as

```
const increase = 12.5/100;
```

but must write instead

```
const increase = 0.125;
```

Exercises for chapter 1

1) Write a program which accepts as input a person's current bank balance and the amount of a withdrawal. The program should print his new balance.

2) A student has taken four examination papers. Write a program which reads his four marks (integers) and prints his average mark.

3) A pay rise of 12.5% has been awarded to a company's employees and is to be backdated for 7 months. Write a program to which an employee can supply as input his previous annual salary and which will inform him how much additional backdated pay he should receive.

4) When a company's employee retires, he will be entitled to an annual pension of one fiftieth of his current annual salary for each complete year's service with the company. Write a program into which an employee can type his current annual salary and the number of complete years he has served with the company. The program should inform him what his annual pension should be.

5) Write a program which reads two integers and reports their sum and product in the form of two equations.

For example, if the input is:

4  7

the output should be

4 + 7 = 11
4 * 7 = 28

6) Write a program which reads the gross price of an item sold and a discount rate (as a percentage). The program should print a sales invoice, for example:

```
************************
gross price      $56.25
discount rate     2.5%
discount        $ 1.41
discount price  $54.84
************************
```

7) Write a program which reads a standard hourly rate of pay, number of ordinary hours worked, and number of overtime hours worked. The overtime rate is 1.5 times the standard rate. Write a program which prints a payslip for the employee concerned.

8) Write a program which draws a Christmas tree outline using asterisks and which displays the message 'a merry christmas' in the centre of the tree.

9) Write a program which prints your first initial in the form of a letter several lines high, for example:

```
        JJ
        JJ
        JJ
        JJ
   JJ   JJ
   JJJJJ
    JJJJ
```

10) Write a program which reads a person's income for a year and his total tax allowance. Assuming all his taxable income is to be taxed at a standard rate, the program should print a tax bill.

# 2 Doing calculations

Doing arithmetic calculations is one of the functions frequently performed by a computer. This chapter tells you more about how to write instructions to make the computer do arithmetic.

## 2.1 Assignment statements

To put a value or number into a variable we can write:

```
read(x)
```

If the value 3 is supplied as input when the program is obeyed, this value is placed in the variable named "x":

x   | 3 |

The statement

```
x := 3
```

also places 3 in the variable "x". This is known as an assignment statement because it assigns a value to the variable. The symbol ":=" should be read as "becomes equal to" and is not to be interpreted as an ordinary equals sign which is used in a totally different context as we shall see later. The left-hand side of an assignment statement must be the name of a variable to which the right-hand side is to be assigned. In the simplest cases, the right-hand side can be a constant as in the above example or another variable name:

```
x := y
```

In this example the contents of "y" are put into "x" (the previous contents of "x" being destroyed or overwritten).

Thus if before the statement is obeyed we have:

x | 2 |     y | 3 |

After the statement is obeyed we have:

x | 3 |     y | 3 |

Note that the value in "y" is left unchanged. We do not **take out** the value in "y", but **copy** it into "x".

## 2.2 The use of simple arithmetic expressions

The right-hand side of an assignment statement can in fact be any arithmetic expression:

```
x := y + z
```

If before the above statement is obeyed we have:

x | 3 |     y | 4 |     z | 5 |

then immediately after the statement is obeyed we have:

x | 9 |     y | 4 |     z | 5 |

Note that a statement such as:

```
x := x + y
```

which, if you are used to algebraic equations, may seem somewhat peculiar, is perfectly valid and means: the value of "x" becomes equal to what it was before plus the value of "y". The right-hand side of an assignment statement is always evaluated first regardless of what variable appears on the left.

Thus if we have:

x [ 3 ]     y [ 4 ]

then immediately after the above statement is obeyed we have:

x [ 7 ]     y [ 4 ]

Now consider part of a program which finds the sum and average of three numbers:

```
read(x, y, z);
writeln('sum is ', x + y + z,
        '. average is ', (x + y + z)/3)
```

This would be better written as:

```
read(x, y, z);
sum := x + y + z;
writeln('sum is ', sum, '. average is ', sum/3)
```

In the second version the expression "x + y + z" is evaluated only once instead of twice and the second version is easier to read. As the programs you write get more complicated you should tend to organize your programs in this way. Note that in this case we could also have written:

```
x := x + y + z
```

or

```
y := x + y + z
```

and avoided using the extra variable "sum". However this would detract from the readability of the program.

### Program 2.1
This program makes use of the extra variables "perimeter" and "floorarea" to hold the value of arithmetic expressions which would otherwise be recalculated.

```
program roomsize3(input,output);

var length, width, height,
    perimeter, floorarea : integer;

begin

    writeln('type in length, width and height');
    read(length, width, height);

    perimeter := 2*(length + width);
    floorarea := length*width;
    writeln('perimeter is ', perimeter);
    writeln('wall area is ', perimeter*height);
    writeln('floorarea is ', floorarea);
    writeln('room volume is ', floorarea*height)

end.
```

## 2.3 More about arithmetic expressions – order of evaluation

In arithmetic expressions above we have sometimes used round brackets. For example:

```
average := (x + y + z)/3
```

or

```
perimeter := 2*(length + width)
```

In each case we have used the brackets to clarify our intentions. We want the computer to calculate:

$$\frac{x + y + z}{3}$$

so we write:

(x + y + z)/3

This is simply a consequence of the fact that we are using a keyboard and arithmetic expressions must be typed as a sequence of characters one after another.

If we missed out the brackets:

```
average := x + y + z/3
```

the computer would calculate:

$$x + y + \frac{z}{3}$$

which is not what we intended.

In the other example, if we removed the brackets:

```
perimeter : = 2*length + width
```

the computer would calculate:

```
(2*length) + width
```

You can see from this that the computer has rules for dealing with the evaluation of arithmetic expressions.

Let us begin by listing the operators that have been informally introduced so far:

```
+    addition
-    subtraction
*    multiplication
/    division
```

The computer can perform only one of these operations at a time. To perform an operation it requires two operands, which are the quantities on either side of the operator. In the absence of brackets, multiplication and division are carried out before addition and subtraction.

Consider the expression:

```
a/b + c/d*e
```

The computer evaluates this as follows:

24

```
          a/b    +    c/d    *    e
           |            |
          1st          2nd
                        |
                    ---3rd---
                  |
          ------4th------

1st result evaluated    a/b
2nd result evaluated    c/d
3rd result evaluated    2nd result * e
4th result evaluated    1st result + 3rd result
```

Thus the computer evaluates:

$$\frac{a}{b} + \frac{c}{d} * e$$

If instead we wanted the computer to evaluate

$$\frac{a}{b} + \frac{c}{d * e}$$

then we would use brackets as follows:

a/b + c/(d*e)

Anything inside brackets is evaluated first. For the operators introduced so far, we can summarise this order of **priority,** as it is called, as follows:

```
order of priority:    1st    anything inside brackets
                      2nd    multiplication and division
                      3rd    addition and subtraction
```

Adjacent operators of the same priority are applied from left to right.

Program 2.2

This program reads into the three variables "dist1", "dist2" and "dist3" the three distances between four towns along a railway line. Given a start time and an average speed in m.p.h. the program prints the time of arrival at each town (assuming stopping time is negligible). Distances are expressed to the nearest mile and the speed as a whole number of m.p.h. Times are expressed as a real number of hours after midnight. e.g. 8.75 means 0845 am. We assume that the journey takes place all on one day.

```
program times(input,output);

var dist1, dist2, dist3, mph          : integer;
    startime, timeat1, timeat2, timeat3 : real;

begin
    read(startime, dist1, dist2, dist3, mph);

    timeat1 := startime + dist1/mph;
    writeln('time of arrival at town 1 is ', timeat1);

    timeat2 := startime + (dist1 + dist2)/mph;
    writeln('time of arrival at town 2 is ', timeat2);

    timeat3 := startime + (dist1 + dist2 + dist3)/mph;
    writeln('time of arrival at town 3 is ', timeat3)

end.
```

We shall see later in this chapter how to handle input and output
of times in hours-and-minutes form.


Program 2.3
This is a more efficient version of Program 2.2. Efficiency in
this context means that this program, which has an effect
identical to Program 2.2, involves fewer arithmetic calculations.
Program 2.2 involves six additions and three divisions whereas
Program 2.3 involves three additions and three divisions. This
sort of consideration beomes important in large programs.

```
program times2(input,output);

var dist1, dist2, dist3, mph  : integer;
    startime, timesofar       : real;

begin

    read(startime, dist1, dist2, dist3, mph);

    timesofar := startime + dist1/mph;
    writeln('time of arrival at town1 is ', timesofar);

    timesofar := timesofar + dist2/mph;
    writeln('time of arrival at town2 is ', timesofar);

    timesofar := timesofar + dist3/mph;
    writeln('time of arrival at town3 is ', timesofar)
end.
```

Instead of using the three variables "timeat1", "timeat2", and
"timeat3", we use a single variable which gets bigger and  bigger

as the program is obeyed. At each step, we are saying: "timesofar" becomes equal to its previous value plus the new time interval.

## 2.4 Special integer operators

There are two special arithmetic operators:

1)   div   which operates only on integers and has the same effect as normal division except that any fractional part is removed, thus producing an integer result.

and   2)   mod   which supplies the remainder after division of two integers.

div and mod have the same priority as "*" and "/".

Consider the following examples:

| expression | value |
|---|---|
| 16/5 | 3.2 |
| 16 div 5 | 3 |
| 16 mod 5 | 1 |
| 19/5 | 3.8 |
| 19 div 5 | 3 |
| 19 mod 5 | 4 |
| 8 div 3 * 3 | 6 |
| 7 + 5 div 3 | 8 |
| 13 - 5 mod 3 | 11 |

The behaviour of these operators on negative operands varies from one PASCAL system to another and should not be relied upon.

## Program 2.4

This is a supermarket "checkout" program which prints the number and denomination of coins required to make up the change from £1 for a purchase costing less than £1 (a whole number of pennies). The program indicates the number of 50p, 10p, 5p, 2p, and 1p coins to be paid out.

```
    program change(input,output);

    var  price, change, noof50s, noof10s,
         noof5s, noof2s, noof1s : integer;

    begin
       read(price);

       change   := 100 - price;
       noof50s  := change div 50;
       change   := change mod 50;

       noof10s  := change div 10;
       change   := change mod 10;

       noof5s   := change div 5 ;
       change   := change mod 5 ;

       noof2s   := change div 2 ;
       change   := change mod 2 ;

       noof1s   := change;

       writeln('change due is: no of 50s     ', noof50s);
       writeln('               no of 10s     ', noof10s);
       writeln('               no of  5s     ', noof5s);
       writeln('               no of  2s     ', noof2s);
       writeln('               no of  1s     ', noof1s)

    end.
```

We have now introduced six arithmetic operators and two of these
can be applied only to integer quantities. A complete list of
operators (some of which have not yet been introduced) is given in
Appendix 2.


## 2.5 More about integer and real variables

At this point some further notes on the differences between
integer and real variables is appropriate. You have already seen
that we distinguish between variables which are going to contain
integer numbers and variables which are going to contain real
numbers. For example:

```
    var numberchildren, numberfamilies : integer;
        childrenperfamily : real;

    begin
           .
           .
           .
        childrenperfamily := numberchildren/numberfamilies;
           .
           .
           .
```

Although "numberchildren" and "numberfamilies" will have integer values, the result of applying the operator "/" is classified as a real quantity - it may have a fractional part - and "childrenperfamily" must therefore be declared as a real variable. In general, you should ensure that integer variables are used for values which can only be whole numbers and real variables are used for values which may have a fractional part.

The classification of a variable as "integer" or "real" is called its **type**. In PASCAL there are many types we can use to classify variables. Up to now we have introduced only two, but others will be introduced later. The computer uses this type information to detect errors made by the programmer, and this is why it is so important to use types accurately. If a programmer says he wants to put to put oranges into a box which he specified earlier was to contain only apples, then the computer can inform the programmer that he has made a mistake. It is a way of building automatic protection into a program.

For example, if you write

```
    var numberchildren, numberfamilies,
                    childrenperfamily : integer;

    begin
        .
        .
        childrenperfamily := numberchildren/numberfamilies;
        .
        .
        .
```

the computer will inform you that you have made a type error and the program would not be run. In this example you have asked the computer to assign a real quantity to an integer variable.

Finally you should remember that the computer stores integer numbers and real numbers in a different way. Although this is normally of little concern to the programmer, it does mean that the largest real number the computer can handle is much bigger than the largest integer number. You should look in your manufacturer's literature for information on the size of integers and real numbers that can be handled. The largest positive integer may only be 32767 on a small computer or more than 2000000000 on others. The largest real number that can be handled will usually have at least 40 digits, but only the first 7 to 15 digits will be accurate (7 on some small computers, 15 or more on large ones).

## 2.6 Standard functions

A number of predefined mathematical operations or functions are available for use in expressions. The programs for evaluating these standard functions have already been written and are stored as part of your PASCAL system.

For example

```
x := 4.0;
writeln( sqrt(x) )
```

prints the value 2.00;

and

```
y := 5.66;
writeln( trunc(y) )
```

prints the value 5.

"sqrt" is the name of the standard function which performs the
operation "finding the square root of". "trunc" is the name of the
standard function which performs the operation "truncate", i.e. it
removes the fractional part from a real number to give an integer.

When you refer to a function you use its name and enclose
within round brackets the value to which the function is to be
applied. This value, which is called a parameter, can be any
arithmetic expression of a type appropriate for the particular
function.

For example:

```
x := sqrt(16);
        .
        .
        .
x := sqrt(y);
        .
        .
        .
x := sqrt(3*y/z);
        .
        .
        .
x := 15.6 + sqrt(3*y/z);
        .
        .
        .
```

Because parameters can be arithmetic expressions, a function can
be used in the expression which is the parameter of another
function:

```
writeln( trunc(sqrt(17.3)))
```

prints 4

```
writeln( sqrt(sqrt(16)))
```

prints 2.00

```
theta := 3.142/3;
writeln(sqrt(sin(theta) + cos(theta)))
```

prints 1.17

You must ensure that the parameter given to a function, whether it is a constant, a variable, or an expression, has the required type. If you are assigning the result of a function to a variable, the type of the variable must correspond to the type of the function result.

For example you cannot write:

```
var x : integer;

begin
    x := sqrt(16);
         .
         .
         .
```

because the type of the result of "sqrt" is classified as real.

There is a complete list of standard functions in Appendix 3, together with information on the types of parameters required and the types of results produced.

Program 2.5
For a standard "inverted v" shaped roof, this program works out the area of roof covering required, given the length and width of the building and the angular pitch of the roof.

```
program roof(input,output);

var pitch, length, width, areaofroof : real;

begin

    writeln('type in pitch of roof(degrees),',
            ' length and width');
    read(pitch, length, width);

    pitch := pitch * 3.14159/180;
    areaofroof := width/cos(pitch) * length;

    writeln('area of roof covering required is ',
            areaofroof, ' sq.m.')

end.
```

You should note that while people usually work in degrees, the parameters of trigonometric functions in PASCAL have to be given in radians, hence the conversion in the above example.


Program 2.6
Converts degrees Centigrade to degrees Fahrenheit.

```
program conversion(input,output);

var cdegrees, fdegrees : real;

begin
    read(cdegrees);
    fdegrees := cdegrees * 9/5 + 32;
    writeln(cdegrees, 'c = ', fdegrees, 'f or approx ',
                      round(fdegrees), 'f')
end.
```

This will produce, for example:

21.50c = 70.70f or approx 71f

Let us now return to a problem raised by program 2.2 and see how we can cope with expressing times such as 12.95 hours after midnight as 1257. One way of doing this is illustrated in the following program:

## Program 2.7

Given a distance between two towns, a speed in miles per hour and a departure time from one town, the program prints the arrival time at the other town. Times are input as, for example, 0845 or 1357 and are output as, for example, 8-45 and 13-57. We again assume that the journey takes place in one day.

```
program journey(input,output);

var dist, mph, startime, hours, mins : integer;
    realhours : real;

begin

    read(dist, mph, startime);

    hours    := startime div 100;
    mins     := startime mod 100;
    realhours:= hours + mins/60;

    (* next statement calculates time of arrival *)
    (* as a real number of hours after midnight *)

    realhours:= realhours + dist/mph;

    (* time now converted back into hours and mins *)

    hours    := trunc(realhours);
    mins     := round((realhours - hours)*60);
    write(' arrival time: ', hours, '-', mins)

end.
```

One further feature has been introduced in the above program. We have inserted comments which explain to the human reader what the program is supposed to be doing. Any group of characters enclosed between (* and *) are printed as part of the program but have no effect on its behaviour when it is obeyed. Such comments should be inserted in a program wherever they make the program easier for the human reader to understand. This would be important if someone else is likely to have to take over your program and modify it, or if you yourself are likely to have to modify it at some future date when the details of how it works have been forgotten.

## 2.7 Raising a number to a power

Finally note that for various reasons there is no "raising to the power of" operator in PASCAL. If we wanted to raise "x" to the 8th power for example, we could write:

```
x := sqr(sqr(sqr(x)))
```

and to the 9th power:

```
x := x*sqr(sqr(sqr(x)))
```

More generally, "x" to the power 3.4 could be calculated by:

```
x := exp(3.4*ln(x))
```

Exercises for Chapter 2

1) Write a program that, given a number as input, prints its square, cube and fourth power without doing any unnecessary calculations.

2) A pay rise of 9.9% has been awarded to a company's employees. Write a program to which an employee can supply as input his previous annual salary and which will inform him of his new annual, monthly and weekly rates of pay. (Assume that there are exactly 52 weeks in the year.)

3) A sum of money has been invested at an annual rate of interest of 14.75%. Interest is calculated and added to the account at the end of each complete year. Write a program which reads the initial amount invested and which prints the balance in the account at the end of each of the first three years.

4) A retiring employee is entitled to an annual pension of one fiftieth of his current annual salary for each complete year's service with the company. All employees start work on the first day of a month and retire on the last day of a month. Write a program into which an employee can type his current annual salary, the month and year he started work with the company, and the month and year he retired. (A month is supplied as an integer in the range 1..12.) The program should inform him what his annual pension will be.
Hint: Calculate the total number of months worked and use div to find the number of complete years worked.

5) A car hire company calculates the charge for the hire of a car using a standard rate for each mile travelled together with a "wear and tear" surcharge for each complete 1000 miles travelled. Write a program which accepts as input the milometer readings at the start and finish of a hire and calculates the total charge for the hire.

6) The floor of a room is to be covered with tiles of dimension 15cm square. There is to be a gap of 2mm between tiles when laid. Write a program that given the room dimensions (in metres) works out the number of whole tiles required. (Calculation of the number of extra tiles required for cutting is somewhat tricky and is left for a later chapter).

7) Write a program which accepts as input the amount of cash (a real number of pounds or dollars) to be enclosed in an employee's pay packet. The program should do a "coin and note analysis" and print the number of coins and notes, of each available denomination, which are to be included in the pay packet.
Hint: Use the techniques illustrated in Program 2.7 to separate the cash amount into pounds and pence, or dollars and cents. Then deal separately with the two amounts as illustrated in Program 2.4.

8) Given a departure and arrival time based on the 24 hour clock and input as in Program 2.7, write a program which will print the duration of the journey (assumed to take place all in one day). Now assume that the departure and arrival times are quoted according to two different time zones, and modify the program to accept a third input that is a positive or negative time margin (a whole number of hours) which is to be applied to the arrival time before doing the above calculation. (Again assume that no change of day takes place).

# 3 Simple loops

Here we encounter our first **control statement.** A control statement is a statement that we can use to change the order in which the various parts of a program are executed. In this chapter we introduce a mechanism which will allow us to make better use of the vast speed at which a computer can operate – a simple loop facility with which we can tell the computer to obey a section of program over and over again.

## 3.1 Preliminary example

It is important at this stage to realize that a variable is just what the term **variable** says it is – its value can change while a program is being obeyed. Consider the following program.

Program 3.1
Adds three numbers together.

```
program add3(input,output);

var next, sum : integer;

begin
    sum:=0;

    read(next);
    sum := sum + next;

    read(next);
    sum := sum + next;

    read(next);
    sum := sum + next;

    writeln(sum)
end.
```

Let us assume that the program is provided with input:

36   7   19

When the first two statements have been obeyed, we have the situation:

sum  | 0 |          next  | 36 |

When the assignment statement on the next line is obeyed, the expression on the right is evaluated first, regardless of what appears on the left. At this stage "sum + next" has the value 36 and this value is placed in the variable "sum", destroying or overwriting the value previously stored there:

sum  | 36 |          next  | 36 |

The next read statement causes the next number in the input to be stored in the variable "next", again overwriting the value previously stored there. "sum + next" now has the value 43 and the next statement places this value in "sum".

sum  | 43 |          next  | 7 |

After obeying the next two statements we have the situation

sum  | 62 |          next  | 19 |

Thus "sum" holds four different values while the program is being obeyed and "next" holds three. The net effect of the program is to add together the three numbers presented in the input. This is done by repeatedly obeying the two statements

```
read(next);
sum := sum + next
```

## 3.2 Simple for-statements

We now present the first of the three looping statements available in PASCAL. These are all used to tell the computer to obey a group of one or more statements again and again. Instead of writing the above three statements in full three times, we can tell the computer to obey these statements three times by using a for-statement:

Program 3.2
Equivalent in effect to Program 3.1.

```
program add3(input,output);

var next, sum, count : integer;

begin
  sum:=0;

  for count:= 1 to 3 do

  begin
    read(next);
    sum:= sum + next
  end;

  writeln(sum)
end.
```

There are several points to note here:

1) The for-statement tells the computer to obey the statement after the word do three times before carrying on to the next statement.

2) After the word do, begin and end have been used to bracket a group of statements to show that they belong together and are to be thought of as a single **compound statement.** Between begin and end we always have a list of statements (two in this case), separated from each other by semicolons. Thus, in this example, the complete sequence of statements between the inner begin and end is obeyed three times before the write-statement is obeyed.

3) "count" is an integer variable which is given the value 1 the first time the compound statement is obeyed, 2 the second time and 3 the third time. The computer uses this variable to count the number of times the compound statement has been obeyed. "count" is called the **control variable** of the for-statement. Until we get to chapter 7, the control variable will always be an integer variable and must be declared as such. As you will see shortly, there is no special significance in the name "count" - we could have given the control variable any name we chose.

4) Remember that a semicolon is used to separate one complete statement from the next. There is no semicolon after do in the above example because the for-statement is not complete until the end of the statement after do. A semicolon is used after the compound statement to separate the completed for-statement from the write statement on the next line.

The behaviour of the for-statement when obeyed can be illustrated diagrammatically by

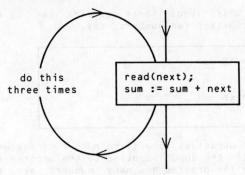

do this
three times

```
read(next);
sum := sum + next
```

hence the use of the term **loop**.

It is instructive to consider the effect of omitting the begin and end brackets after the do in the above program.

```
sum:=0;

for count := 1 to 3 do
    read(next);

sum := sum + next
```

Only the statement following do is obeyed repeatedly and in the absence of begin and end this consists only of

```
read(next)
```

Thus the above is equivalent in effect to

```
sum:=0;
read(next);
read(next);
read(next);
sum := sum + next
```

This reads a number into "next", then reads another, overwriting the previous one, then reads a third. Only the third number is added onto the variable "sum".

It is sensible to type the program in such a way that the meaning is made clear to the human reader. A few extra spaces are usually inserted before the lines containing statements which are to be obeyed repeatedly, thus making these statements stand out in the text. You should remember, however, that this use of layout

39

does not affect the meaning of the program as far as the computer is concerned.

Our for-statement which adds three numbers can be easily modified so as to add together ten numbers, say.

```
for count := 1 to 10 do
begin
    read(next);
    sum := sum + next
end
```

We need not even commit ourselves to a fixed number of values to be added together. If the input supplied to the program starts with an integer telling the program how many numbers are to be added together, we could write

```
read(numberofvalues);  sum := 0;

for count := 1 to numberofvalues do
begin
    read(next);  sum := sum + next
end
```

This program would then accept input such as

5       26  72  41  32  61

and would add together the last 5 numbers. Input of

2       15  42

would result in the addition of the 2 numbers 15 and 42.

## 3.3 Loan repayment example

Now let us revisit the loan repayment example, Program 1.3. An alternative method for calculating and printing the outstanding balance after one repayment would be

```
debt := debt + debt*monthlyrate/100 - payment;
writeln('debt after next payment is ', debt)
```

Here the assignment statement calculates the new balance owing and then stores it in the variable "debt", destroying the previous contents of that variable. The advantage of expressing the calculation in this form is that it can now be obeyed repeatedly as often as we like:

Program 3.3
This program prints a month by month statement for a year's repayments on a loan.

```
program loanrepayment(input,output);

var debt, monthlyrate, payment : real;
    month : integer;

begin
    read(debt, monthlyrate, payment);
    for month := 1 to 12 do
    begin
        debt := debt + debt*monthlyrate/100 - payment;
        writeln('debt after next payment is  ', debt)
    end
end.
```

Given input:

95.00   2   5

this program produces output:

debt after next payment is   91.90
debt after next payment is   88.74
debt after next payment is   85.51
debt after next payment is   82.22
debt after next payment is   78.87
debt after next payment is   75.44
debt after next payment is   71.95
debt after next payment is   68.39
debt after next payment is   64.76
debt after next payment is   61.06
debt after next payment is   57.28
debt after next payment is   53.42

Note that in writing the above program we have assumed that the debt will not be paid off in the first year. If this does happen the computer will still do exactly what we have told it to do. Input of

272   2.5   29

will result in output:

41

```
debt after next payment is   249.80
debt after next payment is   227.04
debt after next payment is   203.72
debt after next payment is   179.81
debt after next payment is   155.31
debt after next payment is   130.19
debt after next payment is   104.45
debt after next payment is    78.06
debt after next payment is    51.01
debt after next payment is    23.28
debt after next payment is    -5.13
debt after next payment is   -34.26
```

We shall see later how we can make the program test for this  sort
of situation and avoid it.


## 3.4 Making use of the control variable

As  we  have  already remarked, the control variable is used by
the computer to count how many times the statement  following  the
do has been obeyed. However, there is no reason why the programmer
should  not  also  make  use  of  the value of this variable. As a
simple example, the statement

```
for i := 1 to 10 do write(i:3)
```

will print the integers from 1 to 10 all on  one  line.  Our  last
program  for  printing a month by month statement for a loan could
make use of the control variable:


Program 3.4
Similar to program 3.3, except that each month number is tabulated
alongside the outstanding debt.

```
program loanstatement(input,output);

var debt, monthlyrate, payment : real;
    month : integer;

begin
    read(debt, monthlyrate, payment);
    writeln('month', 'outstanding debt':19);  writeln;

    for month := 1 to 12 do
    begin
        debt := debt + debt*monthlyrate/100 - payment;
        writeln(month:5, debt:19:2)
    end
end.
```

Given input:

1256.75   1.25   56.50

this program will print

| month | outstanding debt |
|-------|------------------|
| 1 | 1215.96 |
| 2 | 1174.66 |
| 3 | 1132.84 |
| 4 | 1090.50 |
| 5 | 1047.63 |
| 6 | 1004.23 |
| 7 | 960.28 |
| 8 | 915.78 |
| 9 | 870.73 |
| 10 | 825.12 |
| 11 | 778.93 |
| 12 | 732.17 |

The first time the statement

```
writeln(month:5, debt:19:2)
```

is obeyed "month" has the value 1, the second time it has the
value 2 and so on. The formatting information in this statement
has been chosen so that each time the statement is obeyed, the two
values printed are lined up below the two headings which were
output by the statement

```
writeln('month', 'outstanding debt':19)
```

The use of formatting information is explained in Chapter 1,
Section 1.5.

   A program can use a control variable in any way we  like  while
the  corresponding  loop  is being obeyed, except that the program
must not attempt to change the control  variable.  This  would  be
unreasonable  because  it  would  interfere, perhaps disastrously,
with the only record there is of how many times the loop statement
has been obeyed. In  particular,  this means that  inside  the  loop
the control variable must not appear on the left of any assignment
statement or as a parameter of a read-statement. Once the loop has
been  obeyed the appropriate number of times, the control variable
no longer has a defined value, and the  statements  following  the
for-statement  should  not  assume  that it still has a value. The
variable can of course be given a new value or it can be  used  as
the control variable of a subsequent for-statement.

## 3.5 Other features of the for-statement

Some further points about for-statements are illustrated by the following examples.

```
for number := -8 to 5 do write(number:4)
```

When obeyed, this statement will output

```
-8  -7  -6  -5  -4  -3  -2  -1   0   1   2   3   4   5
```

The control variable can go up only in steps of 1. In order to print all the even numbers from 2 to 100 we can use

```
for n := 1 to 50 do writeln(n*2:3)
```

The odd numbers from 1 to 99 could be output by

```
for n := 1 to 50 do writeln(n*2-1:2)
```

or by

```
for n := 0 to 49 do writeln(n*2+1:2)
```

We can use any expression we like to specify the starting and finishing values for the control variable. For example, given two integers m and n (both greater than 1), we can print all the integers from m+n to m*n by

```
for next := m+n to m*n do writeln(next)
```

Finally, the control variable can be made to take values which decrease in steps of 1. For example, we can print the integers from 0 to 100 in reverse order by

```
for k := 100 downto 0 do writeln(k:3)
```

Further use of these possibilities will be illustrated in later chapters.

In general, the for-statement has one of the two forms

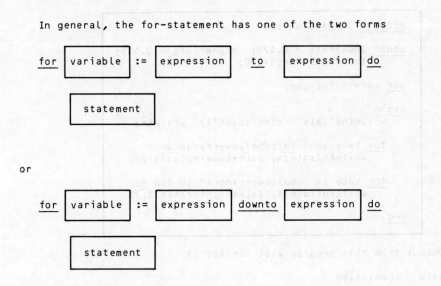

or

## 3.6 Programs with more than one simple loop

The following program contains two for-statements, written one after the other. When the program is obeyed, the first loop will be executed the appropriate number of times before the second is considered. The same control variable is used for both loops, but since only one loop is obeyed at a time, this does not lead to any confusion.

## Program 3.5
A salesman receives commission on his sales at a rate of 12.5% on sales worth $100 or less, and 15.5% on sales worth more than $100. This program prints a table which tells him the value of the commission on any sale up to $200.

```
program commissiontable(output);

const lowerrate = 0.125;  higherrate = 0.155;
      topoflowerrange=100;

var sale : integer;

begin
    writeln('sale    commission');  writeln;

    for sale := 1 to topoflowerrange do
        writeln(sale:4, sale*lowerrate:13:2);

    for sale := topoflowerrange+1 to 200 do
        writeln(sale:4, sale*higherrate:13:2)

end.
```

Output from this program will consist of

| sale | commission |
|------|------------|
| 1 | 0.12 |
| 2 | 0.25 |
| 3 | 0.37 |
| 4 | 0.50 |
| 5 | 0.62 |
| . | . |
| . | . |
| . | . |
| 99 | 12.38 |
| 100 | 12.50 |
| 101 | 15.65 |
| 102 | 15.81 |
| . | . |
| . | . |
| . | . |
| 199 | 30.84 |
| 200 | 31.00 |

The reasons for using named constants in a program like this were discussed in Section 1.6.


Exercises for chapter 3

1) Write a program which reads and adds 15 real numbers and then prints their average.

2) Write a program which reads and multiplies together 20 real numbers.

3) Write a program to print a "4 times table" in the form

46

```
1 x 4 =  4
2 x 4 =  8
3 x 4 = 12
   etc.
```

4) Write a program which reads an integer, n say, and prints an "n times table".

5) Write a program which prints all multiples of 3 from 3 to 90.

6) "n factorial" is defined as n*(n-1)*(n-2)*....*3*2*1. Write a program which reads a value for n and calculates n factorial.

7) Write a program which reads an integer n followed by n real numbers. The program should calculate and print the average of the numbers.

8) The statement "writeln('*':i)" will print a star preceded by i-1 spaces. In fact any integer expression can be used in place of "i". Write a program to read an integer n and print a large "7" occupying n lines. For example, with n=6 output should be

```
******
     *
    *
   *
  *
 *
```

9) Write a program to draw a triangle occupying n lines where n is supplied as input. For example, with n = 4

```
   *
  * *
 *   *
*******
```

10) An electricity board has previous and present meter readings for a known number of customers. Write a program which will read the appropriate number of pairs of readings and print a bill for each customer.

11) 20 candidates have each taken two examination papers, paper 1 and paper 2. The marks obtained are to be typed as input for a computer program. The first two numbers typed are the marks obtained by the first candidate, the next two numbers are the marks obtained by the second candidate, and so on. Write a program which prints the total mark obtained by each candidate over the two exam papers. The program should also calculate and print the overall average mark for paper 1, the overall average mark for paper 2 and the overall average total mark.

# 4 Selecting alternatives

In this chapter, we introduce two more control statements. We can use these to specify alternative courses of action in a program, where the action taken by the computer is to depend on tests made while the program is running.

## 4.1 Selecting one of two alternatives

Here we look at how we can tell the computer to select one of two alternatives. In the first instance we consider that one of the alternatives is to do nothing. A statement is either obeyed or ignored depending on the outcome of a test.

Consider the following simple examples:

```
if age > 18 then
    write('eligible for jury service')
```

```
if weight > 200 then
    write('try slimming')
```

```
if previousconvictions > 3 then
    fine := fine*2
```

```
if total > 100 then
    total := total - 0.10*total
```

In each of these examples the form is:

```
if  condition  then  statement
```

A simple condition relates two quantities using one of a number of relational operators. The particular relational operator we used above was " > " which means "greater than".

The complete list of relational operators is:

| operator | meaning |
|----------|---------|
| > | greater than |
| >= | greater than or equal to |
| < | less than |
| <= | less than or equal to |
| = | equal to |
| <> | not equal to |

The operators >=, <= and <> are single operators written in this way because of the limited number of characters usually available on a keyboard.

The following examples use these operators:

```
if age >= 18 then
    write('eligible for jury service')
```

```
if i <> j then
    write('i and j are unequal')
```

In general, real numbers should not be compared using = or <>. Two values which we think should be identical may differ very slightly when represented inside the computer. For example, because of the limited space available for storing a real, "1/3" might be stored as 0.3333333 and "1/3*3" would therefore be stored as 0.9999999. We can make the computer test whether whether two values are very close to each other by, for example:

```
if abs(x-y) < 0.0001 then
    writeln('x and y are almost equal')
```

The behaviour of a simple if-then statement can be illustrated as follows:

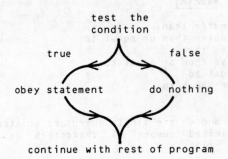

```
                        test   the
                        condition
            true                        false


        obey statement              do nothing


            continue with rest of program
```

The branch taken depends on the outcome of the test. If the condition is satisfied then the left-hand branch is followed, otherwise the right-hand branch is taken. We say that the outcome of a test is the value "true" or the value "false" and this is a concept of which we shall make frequent use later.

Now consider the following examples:

```
if age >= 18 then
    write('eligible for jury service')
else
    write('under age, not eligible for jury service')
```

```
if weight > 200 then
    write('try slimming')
else
    write('your weight is within limit')
```

```
if total > 100 then
    total := total - 0.10*total
else
    total := total - 0.05*total
```

```
if age > 60 then
    benefit := (age - 60)*annualrate
else
    write('no benefit payable')
```

```
if currentreading > previousreading then
    unitsused := currentreading - previousreading
else
    unitsused := 10000 - previousreading + currentreading
```

```
if i <> j then
    write('i and j are unequal')
else
    write('i and j are equal')
```

In each of the above examples the general form is:

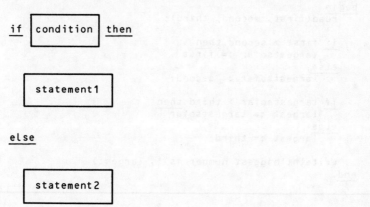

The behaviour of such an if-then-else statement can be illustrated
as follows:

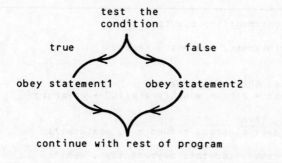

continue with rest of program

    Again  we  are  selecting  one out of two alternatives but this
time the second alternative, instead of being to  do  nothing,  is
another statement. Again the selection is dependent on the outcome
of  the test which can be either "true" or "false". Technically we
say that the condition has a value "true" or  "false".  Statement1

51

is executed if (the value of) the condition is "true", otherwise statement2 is executed because (the value of) the condition is "false".

Here are two complete programs illustrating these mechanisms.

Program 4.1
This program reads three numbers and prints the largest.

```
program largest(input,output);

var first, second, third, largestsofar, largest : real;

begin
   read(first, second, third);

   if first > second then
      largestsofar := first
   else
      largestsofar := second;

   if largestsofar > third then
      largest := largestsofar
   else
      largest := third;

   writeln('biggest number is ', largest)
end.
```

Program 4.2
This program is identical to Program 1.3 except that if the payment is greater than the outstanding debt an appropriate message together with a refund amount is printed.

```
program loanrepayment(input,output);

var debt, monthlyrate, payment : real;

begin
   read(debt,monthlyrate,payment);
   debt := debt + debt * monthlyrate/100 - payment;

   if debt < 0 then
      write('debt cleared. refund = ', abs(debt))
   else
      write('debt after this payment is ', debt)

end.
```

## 4.2 About semicolons

An if-then-else statement is a single statement. Thus a semicolon, which is technically a statement separator, is not inserted before an else. Refer to Program 4.1 which contains two consecutive if-then-else statements. You will see that there is no semicolon before either else but of course a semicolon appears at the end of each if-then-else statement in order to separate it from the next statement. Incidentally, you will find that you **are** permitted to insert a redundant semicolon before an end.

### Program 4.3

Four numbers are input to this program. The first number is interpreted as a standard value and the three further values are compared with this standard value. A message is printed indicating how many of these three values are within 0.1 of the standard value.

```
program tolerance(input,output);

var standard, next : real;  numberclose : integer;

begin
    numberclose := 0;
    read(standard);

    read(next);
    if abs(standard - next) < 0.1 then
        numberclose := numberclose + 1;

    read(next);
    if abs(standard - next) < 0.1 then
        numberclose := numberclose + 1;

    read(next);
    if abs(standard - next) < 0.1 then
        numberclose := numberclose + 1;

    writeln(numberclose,
            ' values are near the standard')
end.
```

For example, if the input is:

3.156    3.051  3.152  3.091

the output will be:

2 values are near the standard


In Program 4.3 the same operations are being performed three times over. A more elegant way of writing this program would be to put the repeated statements inside a loop. We shall do this in

Chapter 6 which deals in detail with the techniques of nesting statements, or putting statements inside other statements.

## 4.3 The use of compound statements

Now it may be that the action to be selected according to the outcome of a test comprises a number of statements rather than a single statement. In this case such statements are bracketed together using the begin...end brackets introduced in Chapter 3.

Program 4.4
This program finds the sum and difference of two numbers ensuring that the larger of the two numbers ends up in variable "larger" and the smaller in variable "smaller". Here we read the two numbers, in the first instance, into variables "larger" and "smaller" and swap the contents of the variables if necessary.

```
program twonumbers(input,output);

var larger, smaller, temporary, sum,
        difference : integer;

begin
    read(larger, smaller);

    if larger < smaller then
    begin
        temporary := larger;
        larger    := smaller;
        smaller   := temporary
    end;

    sum        := larger + smaller;
    difference := larger - smaller;

    writeln('the sum is ', sum);
    writeln('the difference is ', difference);
    writeln('nos. in order are ', larger, smaller)
end.
```

Note that the action to be performed if the outcome of the test is "true" now consists of three statements bracketed together to form a single compound statement. Also note that to swap over the contents of two variables you need three assignment statements and one extra variable. You should examine what would happen if we had written:

```
larger := smaller;
smaller := larger
```

## 4.4 More complicated conditions

The simple conditions we have used so far have been composed of two quantities related by a relational operator:

| quantity1 | relational operator | quantity2 |

The quantities we have used have been variables and constants but they can also be arithmetic expressions:

```
if sum1 + sum2 - credit > 250 then
    write('limit exceeded')
```

```
if age - 60 < 5 then
    benefit := lumpsum * 1.5
else
    benefit := lumpsum
```

```
if total > 1.5 * currentbalance then
    write('limit exceeded')
```

We can combine more than one condition in an if-statement by joining conditions together using the words and and or.

Consider the following examples:

```
if (previousconvictions > 3) and (timespread < 1.5) then
    fine := fine * 4
```

```
if (weight > 200) and (height < 1.7) then
    write('you are overweight')
else
    write('your weight is reasonable')
```

```
if (weight > 200) or (dailycalories > 2000) then
    write('cut down')
else
    write('ok')
```

55

```
if (x=y) and (x > 0) and (y > 0) then
    write('x and y are equal and positive')
```

Note that individual conditions involving relational operators
must be enclosed in round brackets. The words and and or join
individual conditions together to make a more complex condition.
Technically a condition is called a boolean expression.

A common mistake made by new programmers is to write:

```
if (x > 0) and < 10 then......
```

instead of:

```
if (x > 0) and (x < 10) then......
```

You should see from this that each constituent simple condition
involving a relational operator must be complete.


## 4.5 Definition of and and or

When an if-statement contains a condition involving and and or,
the meaning of the condition is usually clear from reading the
program. However, here we tabulate the possible values of a
composite condition involving two subsidiary conditions.

```
        if   condition1   and   condition2   then......


   condition1        condition2        composite condition

    false             false             false
    false             true              false
    true              false             false
    true              true              true
```

```
        if   condition1   or   condition2   then......


   condition1        condition2        composite condition

    false             false             false
    false             true              true
    true              false             true
    true              true              true
```

Try making up your own examples using combinations of and and

56

or. The words and and or are called boolean operators and they
join conditions or boolean expressions together, just as
arithmetic operators join arithmetic expressions together.

    The other boolean operator we use is not. Its use can be
illustrated by a simple example:

```
if not (x = y) then
    write('x and y are unequal')
```

is exactly equivalent to:

```
if (x <> y) then
    write('x and y are unequal')
```

    As with arithmetic operators there is an order of priority. In
the case of boolean operators the order of priority is not, and,
or. Thus:

```
if (calories>2000) or (weight>200) and (height<1.7)  then
    write('you are overeating')
```

is equivalent to:

```
if (calories>2000) or ((weight>200) and (height<1.7)) then
    write('you are overeating')
```

Remember: if in doubt, use extra brackets to make your intentions
clear.


Program 4.5
In this program a person's age is read and a message printed which
indicates whether the person is eligible for jury service or not.

```
program jury(input,output);

var age : integer;

begin
    read(age);

    if (age >= 18) and (age <= 65) then
        writeln('eligible for jury service')
    else
        writeln('not eligible for jury service')
end.
```

57

Alternatively the if-statement could have been written as:

```
if (age < 18) or (age > 65) then
    writeln('not eligible for jury service')
else
    writeln('eligible for jury service')
```

## 4.6 Boolean types and variables

Up to now we have been able to tell the computer that the contents of a storage location or variable are going to be of integer or real type. We now introduce a new type - boolean. A boolean variable can contain only one of the two values "true" or "false". Boolean variables are declared just like other variables:

```
var heavy, bright : boolean;
        .
        .
    heavy := true;
    bright:= false
```

In the above example "heavy" and "bright" are the names of storage locations into which the program places the values "true" and "false" respectively.

heavy | true |     bright | false |

The use of a boolean variable is illustrated by the following fragment of program which prints out part of a menu. The dishes listed on the menu are to vary according to whether or not it is a summer month.

```
var month : integer;  itsasummermonth : boolean;

begin
    read(month);
    itsasummermonth := (month >= 5) and (month <= 8);

    writeln('menu');  writeln;

    if itsasummermonth then writeln('melon')
                       else writeln('oysters');
    writeln;
    write('roast chicken with ');
    if itsasummermonth then writeln('green salad')
                       else writeln('two veg.');
        .
        .
```

When the program is being obeyed, the value of the condition

(month >= 5) and (month <= 8)

is "true" or "false". This value is stored in the boolean variable
"itsasummermonth". The program can then refer to the value of the
condition as often as is necessary without having to perform the
test again. The use of boolean variables in examples like this can
improve the readability of the program, particularly when the
result of a test is to be used more than once. As another example,
consider:

```
var height, weight : real;
    tall,   heavy  : boolean;
begin
    read(height, weight);
    tall  := height > 1.8;
    heavy := weight > 200;

    if tall and heavy then
        writeln('you are big enough to be a policeman.');

    if not tall and not heavy then
        writeln('have you thought about being a jockey?');
        .
        .
        .
```

Program 4.6
An insurance broker wishes to implement the following guidance
table in a program, so that when he types in an age, engine
capacity, and number of convictions the appropriate message is
typed.

| age | engine size | convictions | message |
|-----|-------------|-------------|---------|
| >=21 | >=2000 | >=3 | policy loaded by 45% |
| >=21 | >=2000 | < 3 | policy loaded by 15% |
| >=21 | < 2000 | >=3 | policy loaded by 30% |
| >=21 | < 2000 | < 3 | no loading |
| < 21 | >=2000 | >=3 | no policy to be issued |
| < 21 | >=2000 | < 3 | policy loaded by 60% |
| < 21 | < 2000 | >=3 | policy loaded by 50% |
| < 21 | < 2000 | < 3 | policy loaded by 10% |

```
program policy(input,output);

var over21 , largecar , riskdriver : boolean;
      age , cc , convictions : integer;

begin
  read(age,cc,convictions);

  over21  := age >= 21;
  largecar:= cc >= 2000;
  riskdriver:= convictions >= 3;

    if over21    and       largecar and      riskdriver
    then writeln('policy loaded by 45 percent');

    if over21    and       largecar and not riskdriver
    then writeln('policy loaded by 15 percent');

    if over21    and not largecar and      riskdriver
    then writeln('policy loaded by 30 percent');

    if over21    and not largecar and not riskdriver
    then writeln('no loading');

    if not over21 and       largecar and      riskdriver
    then writeln('no policy to be issued');

    if not over21 and       largecar and not riskdriver
    then writeln('policy loaded by 60 percent');

    if not over21 and not largecar and      riskdriver
    then writeln('policy loaded by 50 percent');

    if not over21 and not largecar and not riskdriver
    then writeln('policy loaded by 10 percent')
  end.
```

It must be pointed out that this is a rather inefficient program
which on average results in a lot of wasteful testing (consider
the case when the last row in the table is to be selected). In
Chapter 6 we will be looking at how we can further develop our if-
then-else structure and a more efficient and more elegant version
of this program will be presented.

There are a number of standard functions which produce as their
result the value "true" or "false". A boolean function can be used
wherever the computer expects a boolean expression. The only
boolean function we mention at this stage is "odd". Its use is
illustrated in the following program fragment:

```
    var i, j, k : integer;

    begin
        read(i);
        if odd(i) then writeln('that integer is odd.')
        else writeln('that integer is even.');

        read(j, k);
        if odd(j) and odd(k) then
            writeln('these two integers are both odd.')
                    .
                    .
                    .
```

## 4.7 Selecting one of many alternatives

There are many contexts in which we require a statement to select one out of a number of alternatives, rather than one out of two alternatives. One way of doing this can be represented diagrammatically as:

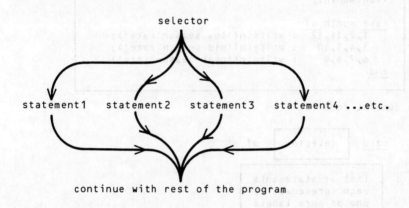

selector

statement1    statement2    statement3    statement4 ...etc.

continue with rest of the program

We have replaced a condition which could have one of two values - "true" or "false" - with a more general selector. The two valued condition which selected one out of two branches has been replaced by an entity which can select one out of a number of branches.
  Consider the following program fragment which could be part of a program for controlling a coin in the slot machine. Depending on the denomination or weight of the coin one out of six totalizing instructions is selected and obeyed.

61

```
    read(weight);

    case weight of
        35 : amountinserted := amountinserted + 50;
        16 : amountinserted := amountinserted + 10;
        9  : amountinserted := amountinserted + 5;
        7  : amountinserted := amountinserted + 2;
        3  : amountinserted := amountinserted + 1;
        1  : amountinserted := amountinserted + 0.5
    end
```

We are assuming that coins of denomination 50,10,5,2,1 and 0.5
have weights of 35,16,9,7,3 and 1 respectively. The structure is
called a case-statement and in this example the selector is (the
value of) "weight" which is an integer variable. "weight" must
contain either 35,16,9,7,3 or 1. If it contains 9 then the third
statement is selected. If it contains 1 then the last statement is
selected. Thus one statement is selected - the statement whose
label corresponds to the value of the selector. More than one
label can be associated with a statement:

```
    read(month);

    case month of
        1,2,11,12 : writeln('low season rate');
        3,4,5,10  : writeln('mid season rate');
        6,7,8,9   : writeln('peak season rate')
    end
```

The general form is:

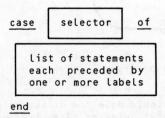

You might wonder what happens if the value of the selector is a
quantity which does not correspond to any label. Say for example
in the coin in the slot program "weight" happened to contain 40.
Well the program will fail and you must ensure that the value of
the selector does correspond to one of the labels. Ways of doing
this are described in Chapter 6.

The selector need not necessarily be a variable, it can be an
arithmetic expression. The next program illustrates a context in
which an expression would be employed. You should note that the
expression must not be real. In the program below the expression
being used as a selector has type integer.

62

Program 4.7
The yearly rate of interest on a loan is:

```
   0 <  loan < 1000  -  10 %
1000 <= loan < 2000  -  11 %
2000 <= loan < 3000  -  11.5 %
3000 <= loan < 4000  -  11.75 %
4000 <= loan < 5000  -  12 %
```

The program works out a year's interest given the size of the
loan. Note that the interest rate could not be conveniently
calculated using a single expression because the variation of rate
with loan size is not linear.

```
program loan(input,output);

var loan , intrate : real;

begin
  read(loan);

  case trunc(loan/1000) of
    0 : intrate := 10   ;
    1 : intrate := 11   ;
    2 : intrate := 11.5 ;
    3 : intrate := 11.75 ;
    4 : intrate := 12
  end;

  writeln('interest to pay: ', loan*intrate/100)
end.
```

If one of the actions to be selected in a case-statement
involves obeying more than one PASCAL statement, then a group of
statements can, as usual, be bracketed together by using
begin...end.

Finally, a boolean expression can be used as a selector in a
case statement. Thus a case statement can be used as an
alternative to an if-then-else statement. For example, in Program
4.1 we could have used

```
case first > second of
   true : largestsofar := first;
   false: largestsofar := second
end;

case largestsofar > third of
   true : largest := largestsofar;
   false: largest := third
end;

writeln('largest value is ', largest)
```

Exercises for Chapter 4

1) Write an electricity bill program similar in specification  to
   Program  1.7  but take into account the fact that a meter goes
   back to zero after reaching 9999 making  the  previous  reading
   greater than the present.

2) Write  a  program  which calculates the discount, if any, on a
   sale. Sales of $100 and over are eligible for a 10% discount.

3) Write a program to accept two items of information: a  British
   shoe  size  and  a 1 or 0 to indicate a man's or woman's shoe.
   The program is to output the American size  according  to  the
   table:

               Men's shoes

       British   7     8     9     10     11
       American  7.5   8.5   9.5   10.5   11.5

               Women's shoes

       British   3     4     5     6      7
       American  4.5   5.5   6.5   7.5    8.5

4) Write  a  program  which  accepts twenty examination marks and
   prints a "pass/fail" message depending on whether  the  average
   is greater than or equal to 50, or less than 50.

5) A  bank  makes a service charge on a customer's account if the
   average daily balance over a 30 day period is less  than  £50.
   The  charge,  if applied, is 20p for each debit entry. Write a
   program which reads  30  pairs  of  values,  where  each  pair
   consists  of  a daily balance and a count of the debit entries
   for the day. The program should  print  a  message  indicating
   whether there should be a service charge, and if so, how much.

6) An  educational  establishment gives 10 courses numbered 1..10.
   Each course is  given  during  two  hourly  periods  and  some
   courses take place concurrently as follows:

64

```
Course 1,2    thu  9am    fri 10am
Course  3     mon 10am    thu 10am
Course 4,5    mon 11am    tue 11am
Course 6,7    tue  9am    wed  2pm
Course  8     mon 12am    thu  9am
Course  9     tue 10am    wed 11am
Course 10     fri  9am    fri 11am
```

Write a timetable enquiry program which is to accept a course number and print a message giving the time periods at which the course is held.

7) At the educational establishment of the previous exercise the days of the week are numbered 1..5 and the hours of each day are numbered 1..6. (Hour 1 is at 9am and Hour 6 is at 2pm). A period is coded as a two digit integer where the first digit gives the day and the second digit gives the hour of a period. Thus, for example, 23 means Tuesday at 11am. Write a program which accepts as input a single integer period code and which outputs the numbers of any courses taking place during that period.

8) Write a program which reads three integers representing an abbreviated date, for example:

26 12 79

and which will print the date in full, for example:

26th december 1979

Note that the day should be followed by an appropriate suffix, 'st', 'nd', 'rd' or 'th'.

9) Write a program which will read the number of a month and, assuming that it is not a leap year, will print the number of days in the month.

10) Extend your solution to Exercise 9 so that it accepts the number of a month and the number of a year (which may be a leap year). It should print the number of days in the month. Note: Your program should start with the statement:

```
if     ((year mod 4 = 0) and (year mod 100 <>0))
       or (year mod 400 = 0)
then daysinfeb := 29
else daysinfeb := 28
```

11) Return to Chapter 2, Exercise 6 and extend your program to calculate the number of extra tiles required for cutting. (Assume that the tiles are not symmetrical, and that a piece cut off a tile at one wall can not be turned through a right angle and used at another wall.)

# 5 Conditional loops

We have seen previously how the computer can be told to obey a section of program a specified number of times. Such a construction is an example of a loop and PASCAL provides two other looping statements which we introduce in this chapter.

## 5.1 Simple repeat-statements

We frequently require the computer to obey a section of program repeatedly until, as a result of this repetition, some condition is satisfied. As a practical analogy, we might instruct a person to keep putting items in a container until the container is full. Consider the following example:

## Program 5.1
A businessman has to make a train journey of about an hour. In order to waste the minimum ammount of time during the day, he wants to have lunch on the train at some time after 12 o'clock. The input for this program consists of a list of the departure and arrival times of suitable trains. These times are in chronological order and are expressed in the 24-hour clock system. The program finds the first train which leaves after 12 o'clock and reports its departure and arrival times.

```
program lunchtrain(input,output);

const startoflunchhour = 1200;

var depart, arrive : integer;

begin

   repeat
      read(depart, arrive)
   until depart >= startoflunchhour;

   write('your train leaves at ', depart);
   writeln(' and arrives at ', arrive)
end.
```

When a repeat-statement is obeyed, the computer starts by obeying any statements between the words repeat and until. The condition after the word until is then tested. Provided the outcome of the test is "false", the statements between repeat and until are

66

obeyed again and the condition tested once more. As long as the outcome of the test is "false", the process is repeated. When the outcome of the test is discovered to be "true", the computer goes on to obey the next statement. This process can be illustrated diagrammatically as follows:

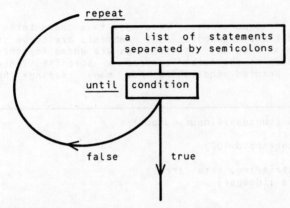

If the timetable contains the following information:

```
0806    0906
0901    0955
1155    1259
1215    1316
1450    1555
1645    1750
```

the output produced will be

your train leaves at 1215 and arrives at 1316

Note that the loop is obeyed only 4 times before the terminating condition is satisfied. Since the read statement is contained within the loop, only the first four lines of the timetable will be required as input by the program.

The above program will be very tedious to use, and rather pointless, if someone has to sit and type the timetable each time the program is obeyed. In most computing systems, it will be possible to type information onto a magnetic disk or tape so that subsequently a program can read the information from disk or tape. The data does not then have to be typed every time the program is obeyed. The way you arrange for a program to do this will depend on the computing system you are using. There will be little or no difference in the program itself, but the commands used to tell the computer to obey the program may change. For the time being, we will continue to assume that all the input for a program is typed at a keyboard while the program is being obeyed, but you should bear in mind the possibility that data read by a program may in fact come from somewhere else and will not necessarily have

67

to be typed afresh every time the program is tested or used.

   In a repeat-statement, the two words repeat and until mark the beginning and end of the section of program which is to be obeyed repeatedly and, if more than one statement appears here, there is no need to bracket them with begin and end:

Program 5.2
A sequence of experimental readings have been taken at daily intervals and these readings, (real numbers), are to be typed as input to this program. The readings are added together, one by one, and as soon as the total exceeds a specified threshold a message is printed indicating how many readings have been processed.

```
program countdays(input,output);

const threshold=100;

var nextreading, total :real;
    days :integer;

begin
   days := 0;  total := 0;

   repeat
      days := days + 1;
      read(nextreading);
      total := total + nextreading
   until total > threshold;

   writeln('threshold total of ', threshold,
           ' has been exceeded.');
   writeln('this occurred after ', days, ' days.')
end.
```

## 5.2 Simple while-statements

   Let us return to the loan-repayment example discussed in Chapter 3. Suppose we want a program to print a month-by-month statement for the duration of the loan. As before the computer must repeatedly obey the two statements:

```
debt := debt + debt*monthlyrate/100 - payment;
writeln('debt after next payment is ', debt)
```

but only as long as the outstanding debt is greater than the repayment which is about to be made. We could use a repeat-statement as follows:

```
read(debt, monthlyrate, payment);

repeat
    debt := debt + debt*monthlyrate/100 - payment;
    writeln('debt after next payment is ', debt)
until debt + debt*monthlyrate/100 < payment
```

This does not take into account the possibility of the initial
payment being greater than the initial debt plus one month's
interest. Although you may think it unlikely that the program will
be presented with such a situation, a well-written program should
cater for every eventuality. This example is best programmed by
using a while-statement:


Program 5.3
This program prints a month-by-month statement for the duration of
the loan.

```
program completestatement(input,output);

var debt, monthlyrate, payment :real;

begin
    read(debt, monthlyrate, payment);

    while debt + debt*monthlyrate/100 >= payment do
    begin
        debt := debt + debt*monthlyrate/100 - payment;
        writeln('debt after next payment is ', debt)
    end;

    writeln;
    writeln('final payment required will be ',
            debt + debt*monthlyrate/100)
end.
```

When a while-statement is obeyed, the computer starts by testing
the condition after the word while. If the outcome is "true", the
statement after the word do is obeyed and the condition after the
word while is tested again. The process is repeated as long the
outcome of the test is "true". As soon as the outcome of the test
is "false", the computer goes on and obeys the next statement.

69

Diagrammatically we have

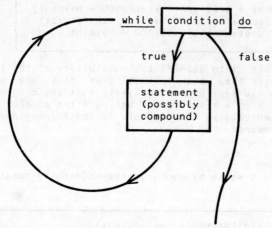

Note that in Program 5.3, the loop statements had to be
bracketed together into a single compound statement by using <u>begin</u>
and <u>end</u>. This is necessary because the condition used to control
the while-statement is written before the loop statement and there
is no natural terminator as there is in a repeat-statement.

Note also that the condition used to control the while-
statement is evaluated before the loop is obeyed for the first
time, and the loop may therefore not be obeyed at all.

In Program 5.3, the expression "debt + debt*monthlyrate/100"
was evaluated twice for each execution of the loop. We shall see
how to avoid this in Section 5.5.

## 5.3 <u>Comparison</u> <u>of</u> <u>repeat-statements</u> <u>and</u> <u>while-statements</u>

In the following table we summarize the main differences
between repeat-statements and while-statements.

| <u>repeat</u> | <u>while</u> |
|---|---|
| The loop statements are obeyed at least once. | The loop statements may not be obeyed at all. |
| When the loop condition is "true", the computer stops obeying the loop. | As long as loop condition is "true" the computer keeps obeying the loop. |
| The words <u>repeat</u> and <u>until</u> act as brackets between which we can write as many statements as we like. | If more than one statement is to be obeyed repeatedly these must be bracketed together between <u>begin</u> and <u>end</u> |

In some examples, the choice of which statement to use is largely a matter of personal taste. For example, the loop in Program 5.2 could have been equally well expressed as

```
while total <= threshold do
begin
    days := days + 1;
    read(nextreading);  total := total + nextreading
end
```

In such cases, the authors prefer the use of the repeat-statement.

In some examples where we could use either statement, the use of a while-statement is a little clumsy. For example, in order to express the loop of Program 3.1 using a while-statement, we need to insert an extra read statement in order that the while condition can be evaluated before the loop has been obeyed for the first time:

```
read(depart, arrive);
while depart <= startoflunchhour do
    read(depart, arrive)
```

Note that begin...end are not necessary in this example, as only a single statement is being obeyed repeatedly.

Finally, there are some examples in which only the while-statement is satisfactory. This was the case in Program 3.3 and the following example illustrates another such situation.

Program 5.4
This program types out a simple sum for the person sitting at the keyboard to attempt. The program then reads the answer which is typed. As long as the answer is wrong, the person sitting at the keyboard is asked to try again. An appropriate message is output when the correct answer has eventually been typed.

```
program arithmetictest(input,output);

const a = 16;  b = 25;

var nooftries, answer :integer;

begin
    writeln('lets test your arithmetic.');
    writeln('type the answer to the following sum.');
    write(a, ' + ', b, ' = ');
    read(answer);  nooftries :=1;

    while answer <> a+b do
    begin
        writeln;  writeln('wrong - try again.');
        write(a, ' + ', b, ' = ');
        read(answer);  nooftries := nooftries + 1
    end;

    writeln;
    if nooftries = 1 then
        writeln('very good, got it in one!')
    else writeln('got it at last!');
    writeln('bye for now!')
end.
```

When executed, this program might produce a display such as

```
lets test your arithmetic.
type the answer to the following sum.
16 + 25 = 42

wrong - try again.
16 + 25 = 41

got it at last!
bye for now!
```

The numbers 42 and 41 have been typed by the user, and the rest by
the  program. If the user types the correct answer the first time,
it would clearly be unsatisfactory for the statements in the  loop
to  be  obeyed  at all.  This  is a trivial example of a Computer
Assisted Learning (CAL) program. A more  realistic  program  would
generate  random  numbers for "a" and "b" and would then use these
numbers.


## 5.4 Multiple terminating conditions

In Programs 3.3 and 3.4 we printed a  month-by-month  statement
for  the  first  12 monthly repayments of a loan. As we mentioned,
these programs will produce nonsensical results  if  the  loan  is
paid  off  in  less than a year. Program 5.3 ensures that the debt
does not become negative, but insists on printing a  statement  for
the  duration of the loan, however long that may be. The following
program combines the two different stopping conditions:

72
```
```

Program 5.5
This prints a month-by-month statement for the first 12 monthly repayments of a loan, or for the duration of the loan if that is less than 12 months.

```
program loanstatement(input,output);

var debt, monthlyrate, payment : real;
    month :integer;

begin
   read(debt, monthlyrate, payment);
   writeln('month   outstanding debt');  writeln;
   month := 0;

   while (month < 12) and
         (debt + debt*monthlyrate/100 >= payment) do
   begin
      month := month + 1;
      debt := debt + debt*monthlyrate/100 - payment;
      writeln(month:5, debt:19:2)
   end;

   writeln;
   if month < 12 then
   begin
      writeln('debt cleared within a year.');
      writeln('final payment: ',
              debt + debt*monthlyrate/100)
   end
end.
```

As another example, consider the problem of a meteorologist who requires programs which can be used to analyze the weather readings for a particular year:

Program 5.6
This reads input which consists of 365 pairs of values, one pair for each day of the year. The first number in each pair is the average temperature for the day and the second is the number of hours of sunshine for the day. The program counts how many days elapsed before the first day on which both the average temperature exceeded 15 degrees and the number of hours of sunshine exceeded 10. The program caters for the possibility that there is no such day.

```
program heatwave(input,output);

const tempthreshold = 15;  sunthreshold =10;

var nexttemp, nextsun :real;
    day :integer;

begin
   day := 0;

   repeat
      day := day + 1;
      read(nexttemp, nextsun)
   until (nexttemp > tempthreshold) and
         (nextsun > sunthreshold) or
         (day = 365);

   if (nexttemp > tempthreshold) and
      (nextsun > sunthreshold)
   then writeln('there were ', day-1,
                ' days before the first good day.')
   else writeln('that was an exceptionally bad year.')
end.
```

In the above example, there are two reasons why the program might
stop obeying the loop. In order to test why the loop terminated
and print an appropriate message, the program had to re-test the
main stopping condition with an if-statement. Note that it would
have been wrong for the if-statement to use the condition
"day <> 365" instead, as this would not result in an appropriate
message in the case where the last day of the year was found to
satisfy the temperature and sunshine requirements. Neater ways of
dealing with this will be discussed later.

## 5.5 Data terminators

We saw in Chapter 3 how we could instruct the computer to read
and process a given number of values supplied as input. In Program
3.2, the number of items to be handled was fixed at three. Each
time this program is obeyed, three values have to be supplied as
input. In Chapter 3, we also demonstrated how the number of values
to be handled could be indicated by a number typed at the start of
a program's input. Each time such a program is obeyed, a different
number of values is processed and the person supplying the input
will have to know how many values there are before he can start
typing the input. This is not always convenient, particularly
where the number of values to be processed is large.

Here we present a widely used alternative approach. The input
starts with the sequence of values to be processed and a special
value is typed at the end of the input to indicate that there are
no further values. Such a special value is called a data
terminator.

This program reads and adds a sequence of positive real numbers (at least one). In this program the data terminator is any negative number.

```
program add(input,output);

var sum, next :real;

begin
    sum := 0;

    read(next);
    repeat
        sum := sum + next;
        read(next)
    until next < 0;

    writeln('sum is ', sum)
end.
```

This program illustrates a common feature of conditional loops: the next value to be processed is obtained at the end of the loop so that this value is tested before it is processed. This necessitates obtaining the first value before entering the loop.

A similar structure is required in Programs 5.3 and 5.5 if we wish to avoid evaluating the expression

    debt + debt*monthlyrate/100

twice during each execution of the loop:

```
read(debt, monthlyrate, payment);

debt := debt + debt*monthlyrate/100;
while debt >= payment do
begin
    debt := debt - payment;
    writeln('debt after next payment is  ', debt);
    debt := debt + debt*monthlyrate/100
end;

writeln('final payment required will be  ', debt)
```

Here we add a month's interest to "debt" at the end of the loop so that this new value of "debt" can be tested before the next payment is subtracted at the beginning of the loop.

It is interesting to consider a number of alternative constructions for the loop in Program 5.7, all of which are occasionally produced by beginners and all of which are **wrong**.

```
sum := 0;
repeat
   read(next);
   sum := sum + next
until next < 0
```

This would add the data terminator, which is a negative number, to the total.

```
sum := 0;
read(next);
repeat
   read(next);
   sum := sum + next
until next < 0
```

This would not add the first number onto the total and would again add the data terminator onto the total.

```
sum := 0;
repeat
   read(next);
   sum := sum + next;
   read(next)
until next > 0
```

This version adds together the first, third, fifth, etc. numbers in the data and tests the second, fourth, sixth, etc.

If the numbers in the input are being handled in groups of two or more, care has to be taken in handling data terminators. The neatest solution is to insert a group of data terminators which contains the same number of values as the groups into which the rest of the data is organized:

Program 5.8
Voting takes place for two political parties in a number of constituencies. The two vote-totals for each constituency are typed in pairs as input to a program and two negative numbers are typed in the input when all pairs of totals have been typed. This program adds up the overall totals for the two parties and reports the overall result.

```
program election(input,output);

var party1next, party2next,
    party1overall, party2overall :integer;

begin
    party1overall := 0;  party2overall := 0;

    read(party1next, party2next);
    repeat
        party1overall := party1overall + party1next;
        party2overall := party2overall + party2next;
        read(party1next, party2next)
    until party1next < 0;

    writeln('party1: ', party1overall, '   ',
            'party2: ', party2ovarall)
end.
```

If presented with input:

```
 3  7
 5  9
 4  2
-1 -1
```

this program will output

party1: 12    party2: 18

The logical structure of this program is the same as that of
Program 5.7, except that the input values are processed in pairs.
Two data terminators are needed in order that they can be read by
the same statement that reads the other pairs of values. (The test
for termination of the loop needs to examine only the first value
of each pair.) If we wish to type only one negative value at the
end of the input data, a slightly more difficult structure is
required for the loop:

```
read(party1next);
repeat
    read(party2next);
    party1overall := party1overall + party1next;
    party2overall := party2overall + party2next;
    read(party1next)
until party1next < 0
```

This version reads only one number at the end of the loop and
tests it. Only if this value is not the terminator can a second
value be safely read.

Finally, we present a program in which two repeat-statements
are used one after the other.

Program 5.9
This program adds up the overall totals for the two parties in an election, but the constituency subtotals for one party are all typed first in the input and are terminated by a negative number. The subtotals for the second party are then typed and are also terminated by a negative number.

```
program election2(input,output);

var party1next, party1overall,
    party2next, party2overall :integer;

begin
    party1overall := 0;
    read(party1next);
    repeat
        party1overall := party1overall + party1next;
        read(party1next)
    until party1next < 0;

    party2overall := 0;
    read(party2next);
    repeat
        party2overall := party2overall + party2next;
        read(party2next)
    until party2next < 0;

    writeln('party1: ', party1overall, '    ',
            'party2: ', party2overall)
end.
```

As was the case in Program 3.5, the second loop is not encountered until the first loop has been obeyed the appropriate number of times. The first repeat-loop is obeyed until the first negative number is read and only then can the program carry on to obey the next loop. The input for the program will take the form

```
3  5  4  -1
7  9  2  -1
```

or even

```
2  3  7  9  4  -1
1  7  6  -1
```

if candidates for party 1 are standing for election in more constituencies than are candidates for party 2.

5.6 Use of boolean variables

A boolean variable often provides a neat way for a programmer to express the terminating condition for a loop, and to test subsequently why the loop was terminated. As an example, we shall rewrite Program 5.6 to use a boolean variable in this way.

Program 5.10
An alternative version of Program 5.6 using a boolean variable.

```
program heatwave2(input,output);

const tempthreshold = 15;  sunthreshold =10;

var nexttemp, nextsun :real;
    day :integer;
    warmdayfound :boolean;

begin
    day := 0;
    warmdayfound := false;

    repeat
        day := day + 1;
        read(nexttemp, nextsun);
        warmdayfound := (nexttemp > tempthreshold)  and
                        (nextsun > sunthreshold)
    until warmdayfound or (day = 365);

    if warmdayfound then
        writeln('there were ', day-1,
                ' days before the first good day.')
    else
        writeln('that was an exceptionally bad year.')
end.
```

Further examples of this approach will appear in later chapters.


Exercises for chapter 5

1) A travelling salesman knows that one of his customers will not
   be available to see him until after 10am. He wishes to catch
   the first train which arrives at the customer's station after
   10am. Write a program which reads a day's train timetable as
   used in Program 5.1 and which tells him when his train leaves.

2) An organization has approximately $1000 available to be
   allocated in small amounts to approved charities. The amounts
   approved for each charity are to be typed as input for a
   program in the order in which requests were received. Write a
   program which will read these amounts and report as soon as
   over $1000 has been allocated.

3) The initial amount of a loan, the monthly repayment and the
   monthly rate of interest are known. Write a program which will
   count how many months will elapse before the loan is paid off
   and prints a message indicating the duration of the loan in
   years and months.

4) 365 figures representing the rainfall in millimetres for

consecutive days in a year are available. Write a program which counts how many days elapsed before the total rainfall for the year up to that point exceeded 250 millimetres. Allow for the possibility of a very dry year.

5) Write a program which accepts a person's initial bank balance followed by a sequence of positive and negative real numbers representing transactions. A positive number represents a credit entry in the account and a negative number represents a debit entry. The input is terminated by a zero entry. The program should print the new balance.

6) In a board game for three players, the players take turns at making a move, and a player scores a variable number of points for each move made. The game finishes when one of the players obtains a zero score for his move. Write a program which accepts, as input, the separate move scores and announces each player's total score. Assume that the scores are supplied to the program three at a time, one for each player in the order in which they played. The last group of scores is to be made up to three, if necessary, by the insertion of one or two additional zeros.

7) A machine is manufacturing ball-bearings and, at equal time-intervals during a production run, a ball-bearing is sampled and its diameter measured. A sequence of such measurements terminated by a negative number is available for input to a computer program. A similar sequence of measurements is available from a production run on a second machine. Each ball-bearing should have a diameter of 2.0mm. Write a program which reads the two separate sets of measurements and reports which machine is producing samples whose average diameter is closer to the ideal value.

8) Write a program which accepts as input a set of sample diameter measurements from a production run on one of the machines described in Exercise 7. The program should report whether the sample contained any ball-bearings that were excessively large (>2.05) or excessively small (<1.95). The program should not waste time reading further input if such a value is found in the sample.

80

# 6 Statements within statements

Sometimes a control structure needs to be included inside another. For example it is possible to have a conditional statement inside a loop, a loop within a conditional statement and loops within loops. In this chapter we demonstrate how to write programs involving nested control structures. We shall use examples of some of the most commonly occurring structures.

## 6.1 if-statements within loops

We have seen in Chapter 3 that a for-statement can take the form

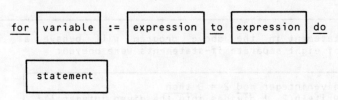

The statement to be obeyed repeatedly can in fact be any PASCAL statement. We now illustrate the case where an if-statement is obeyed repeatedly by writing a program to print all the integers between 2 and 9 which divide exactly into a given integer. We can describe in outline what the program must do as follows:

```
read(giveninteger);

for i := 2 to 9 do

    statement to test whether i divides
    exactly   into   the   given   integer
```

In order to test whether an integer "i" divides exactly into "giveninteger" we can use

```
if giveninteger mod i = 0 then
    writeln(i, ' divides into the given integer.')
```

and this is the statement which must follow the <u>do</u> of the above for-statement:


<u>Program 6.1</u>
To print all the positive integers under 10 which divide exactly into a given number.

```
program factors(input, output);

var giveninteger, i : integer;

begin
    read(giveninteger);

    for i := 2 to 9 do

        if giveninteger mod i = 0 then
            writeln(i, ' divides into the given integer.')

end.
```

The for-statement in the above program will behave as if a sequence of eight separate if-statements were obeyed:

```
if giveninteger mod 2 = 0 then
    writeln(2, ' divides into the given integer.');
if giveninteger mod 3 = 0 then
    writeln(3, ' divides into the given integer.');

if giveninteger mod 9 = 0 then
    writeln(9, ' divides into the given integer.')
```

Thus, given input of 18, the program will print

2 divides into the given integer.
3 divides into the given integer.
6 divides into the given integer.
9 divides into the given integer.


In Program 4.3, the same test was applied to three input values by using three separate occurrences of the same if-statement. Such a process is better structured as a loop:

```
for count := 1 to 3 do

    ┌─────────────────┐
    │ process the next│
    │ value in the input│
    └─────────────────┘
```

The statement following the do can be a compound statement and it
can be as complicated as we like; in this example it must read the
next value in the input and then test it as in the following
version of the program:


Program 6.2
Four numbers are input to this program. The first number is
interpreted as a standard value and the three further values are
compared with this standard value. A message is printed indicating
how many of these three values are within 0.1 of the standard
value.

```
program tolerance2(input,output);

var standard, next : real;
    numberclose, count : integer;

begin

    numberclose := 0;
    read(standard);

    ┌──────────────────────────────────────────────┐
    │ for count := 1 to 3 do                         │
    │ begin                                          │
    │                                                │
    │   ┌──────────────────────────────────────────┐│
    │   │ read(next);                               ││
    │   │ if abs(standard - next) < 0.1 then        ││
    │   │    numberclose := numberclose + 1         ││
    │   └──────────────────────────────────────────┘│
    │                                                │
    │ end;                                           │
    └──────────────────────────────────────────────┘

    writeln(numberclose, ' values are near the standard.')
end.
```

Program 6.3
This is an elaboration of Program 6.2. Numbers are input to a
program from a length-measuring device which measures the length
of a manufactured component on a production line. The program
counts the number of components within 0.1 of a standard length of
6.37 and the number of components outside this tolerance. The
program terminates when it receives any negative number. We
simulate input from the length measuring device by using "read"
and the keyboard.

83

```
program tolerance3(input,output);

const standard = 6.37;
var length : real;
    nowithin, nowithout : integer;

begin

nowithin := 0;
nowithout:= 0;

read(length);

repeat

    if abs(length - standard) < 0.1 then
       nowithin := nowithin + 1
    else
       nowithout:= nowithout + 1;

    read(length)

until length < 0;

writeln(nowithin,  ' values are within  tolerance.');
writeln(nowithout, ' values are outside tolerance.')
end.
```

## 6.2 Loops within Loops

One loop inside another loop is a nested structure frequently encountered in programs. This is because so much data analyzed by computer programs is organized in the form of tables.

Consider the problem of processing the 5 examination marks obtained by each of 25 candidates. The structure required is a loop of the form

```
for candidate := 1 to 25 do

    process the marks obtained
    by  the   next   candidate
```

Processing one candidate's marks might involve reading the 5 marks obtained by the candidate, computing his average and testing for a pass or fail:

```
total := 0;

for exam := 1 to 5 do
begin
    read(mark);
    total := total + mark
end;

average := total/5;
if average >= 50 then
    writeln('passed, average is ', average)
else
    writeln('failed, average is ', average)
```

and a segment of program like this must be obeyed 25 times. This can be achieved by bracketing it into a single compound statement and inserting it into the previous for-statement:


Program 6.4
Data is presented to this program in the form of a table. The table consists of 25 rows of 5 exam marks, each row representing the performance of one candidate in 5 exams. The program outputs a reference number, a pass/fail message and an average mark for each of the 25 candidates.

```
program examarks(input,output);

var candidate, exam, total, mark : integer;
    average : real;
begin

    for candidate := 1 to 25 do
    begin

        total := 0;

        for exam := 1 to 5 do
        begin
            read(mark);
            total := total + mark;
        end;

        average := total/5;
        if average >= 50 then
            writeln('candidate  ', candidate,
                    ' passed, average is ', average)
        else
            writeln('candidate  ', candidate,
                    ' failed, average is ', average)

    end

end.
```

85

In the above program the outer loop is executed 25 times. Once the computer enters the innermost box, which contains another loop, it stays there until this loop has been executed 5 times. The innermost instructions are executed a total of 25x5 times and 125 marks would be supplied as input data in the form of 25 groups of 5 marks. If we imagine a counter associated with each loop then the "exam" counter would be turning 5 times as fast as the "candidate" counter, resetting to 1 for each new candidate.

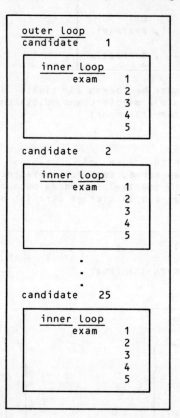

To improve your understanding of the idea of a nested loop, you should examine the difference in behaviour between the following two fragments of program:

```
for i := 1 to 3 do

    for j := 1 to 3 do
        writeln(i, ' ', j)
```

which prints

```
1 1
1 2
1 3
2 1
2 2
2 3
3 1
3 2
3 3
```

and

```
for i := 1 to 3 do
    writeln(i);

for j := 1 to 3 do
    writeln(j)
```

which prints

```
1
2
3
1
2
3
```

The first fragment is of course a nested structure, whereas the
second is just two consecutive loops. As a further illustration,
let us construct a program which will display a triangle of stars
(of a given size) on a background of dots. For example a triangle
of 4 lines would be:

```
.........
....*....
...***...
..*****..
.*******.
.........
```

In outline, the program required will behave as follows:

```
read(noofrows);
calculate width of picture;
for ch := 1 to widthofpicture do write('.');
writeln;

    for rowno := 1 to noofrows do

        print the next row of the triangle with
        the appropriate number of dots on either side;

    for ch := 1 to widthofpicture do write('.')
```

The width of the picture is given by "2*noofrows + 1". Printing a row of the triangle can be described in more detail as:

```
calculate number of stars in this row;
calculate number of background dots at each end of  row;
for ch := 1 to noofdots  do write('.');
for ch := 1 to noofstars do write('*');
for ch := 1 to noofdots  do write('.')
```

The number of stars to be printed on a row is "2*rowno - 1" and the number of background dots required is "noofrows + 1 - rowno". These loops must be nested inside the second loop in the outline above because our triangle is made up of a number of such lines. Filling in these details we get the following program.


Program 6.5
This program displays a triangle of stars on a background of dots.

```
program framedtriangle(input,output);

var noofrows, widthofpicture, ch,
    rowno, noofstars, noofdots : integer;

begin
    read(noofrows);
    widthofpicture := 2*noofrows + 1;
    for ch := 1 to widthofpicture do write('.');
    writeln;

    for rowno := 1 to noofrows do
    begin
        noofstars := 2*rowno - 1;
        noofdots  := noofrows + 1 - rowno;
        for ch := 1 to noofdots  do write('.');
        for ch := 1 to noofstars do write('*');
        for ch := 1 to noofdots  do write('.');
        writeln
    end;

    for ch := 1 to widthofpicture do write('.');
    writeln
end.
```

The final example in this section involves an if-statement inside a repeat-statement inside a for-statement.

Part of a daily sales analysis program involves printing a list of the number of items costing more than $10 that were sold in each of 63 departments:

```
for dept := 1 to 63 do

    analyze the sales for one department
```

The input for each department consists of a list containing the price of each item sold in the department on the day in question, and each list is terminated by -1. One department's sales can therefore be analyzed by:

```
largesales := 0;
read(nextitemprice);

repeat

    test nextitemprice to see if it is a large sale;

    read(nextitemprice)
until nextitemprice < 0;

write number of large sales for this department
```

Filling the rest of the details we obtain:

Program 6.6

```
program salesanalysis(input,output);

var dept, largesales : integer;
    nextitemprice : real;

begin

    for dept := 1 to 63 do
    begin
        largesales := 0;
        read(nextitemprice);

        repeat

            if nextitemprice >= 10 then
                largesales := largesales + 1;

            read(nextitemprice);
        until nextitemprice < 0;

        writeln('dept no. ', dept, ' has made ',
            largesales, ' large sales')

    end

end.
```

89

## 6.3 Nested if-statements

Consider the following sequence of 3 if-statements:

```
if age < 21 then
    writeln('refuse policy');

if age >= 35 then
    writeln('issue policy with discount');

if (age >= 21) and (age < 35) then
    writeln('issue policy at full price')
```

Here three consecutive if-statements are used to select one of three possible courses of action. The three conditions used are such that one and only one of them must be true. However, even if the condition in the first if-statement is true, the computer will still waste time testing the conditions in the remaining two if-statements. If the conditions in the first two if-statements are false, the condition in the third must be true and the computer will again waste time testing it. These inefficiencies can be eliminated by using a more appropriate if-statement structure for making the tests involved. Let us start by noting that if age < 21 then the first write-statement should be obeyed and no further tests made. This can be achieved by using an if-then-else structure which can be outlined as follows:

```
if age < 21 then
    writeln('refuse policy')
else

    statement to be obeyed
    only if age >= 21
```

Any statement inserted after the else will be obeyed only if age >= 21. In this example we can obtain the effect we require by making the statement after the else a further if-statement which distinguishes the cases age >= 35 and age < 35:

```
if age < 21 then
    writeln('refuse policy')
else

    if age >= 35 then
        writeln('issue policy with discount')
    else
        writeln('issue policy at full price')
```

This version of the program will not test the second condition if

90

the first is satisfied and will automatically obey the third write-statement if the first two conditions are false. We can illustrate the behaviour of this nested if-statement as follows:

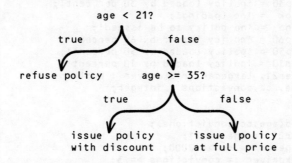

We can imagine the computer following one path from the top of this diagram and carrying out the action at the end of that path.

Program 6.7
This is a more efficient version of Program 4.6, which selected one out of 8 messages to be typed according to 3 items of information input - age, size of car and conviction record.

```
program policy2(input,output);

const p45 = 'policy loaded by 45 percent';
      p15 = 'policy loaded by 15 percent';
      p30 = 'policy loaded by 30 per cent';
      ok  = 'no loading';
      no  = 'no policy to be issued';
      p60 = 'policy loaded by 60 percent';
      p50 = 'policy loaded by 50 percent';
      p10 = 'policy loaded by 10 percent';
var over21, largecar, riskdriver : boolean;
    age, cc,convictions : integer;

begin
   read(age,cc,convictions);
   over21 := age >= 21;
   largecar := cc >= 2000;
   riskdriver := convictions >= 3;

   if over21 then

       if largecar then

           if riskdriver then writeln(p45)
           else               writeln(p15)

       else

           if riskdriver then writeln(p30)
           else               writeln(ok)

   else

       if largecar then

           if riskdriver then writeln(no)
           else               writeln(p60)

       else

           if riskdriver then writeln(p50)
           else               writeln(p10)

end.
```

You should now compare the structure of this program with
Program 4.6, which is identical in effect, and by constructing a
tree diagram appreciate the difference between the two structures.
An alternative way of implementing the nested if-statement in this
program is to use a nested case-statement as follows:

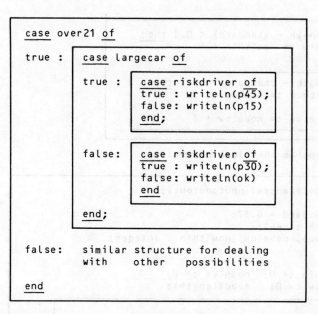

```
case over21 of

true :    case largecar of

          true :    case riskdriver of
                    true : writeln(p45);
                    false: writeln(p15)
                    end;

          false:    case riskdriver of
                    true : writeln(p30);
                    false: writeln(ok)
                    end

          end;

false:    similar structure for dealing
          with    other    possibilities

end
```

The next program illustrates the use of a nested if-statement within a loop.

Program 6.8
This is an elaboration of Program 6.3. The program counts the number of components within 0.1 of a standard length of 6.37, the number of components whose length is too high and the number whose length is too low. As before, we have the outline structure:

```
read(length);
repeat

   test length;

   read(length)
until length < 0
```

To test a length, we require to distinguish three separate possibilities as follows:

93

```
if abs(length - standard) < 0.1 then
    nowithin := nowithin + 1
else

    if length - standard >= 0.1 then
        noabove := noabove + 1
    else
        nobelow := nobelow + 1
```

The complete program therefore becomes:

```
program tolerance4(input,output);

const standard = 6.37;
var length : real;
    noabove, nobelow, nowithin : integer;

begin
    nowithin := 0;  noabove := 0;
    nobelow := 0;   read(length);

    repeat

        if abs(length - standard) < 0.1 then
            nowithin := nowithin + 1
        else

            if length - standard >= 0.1 then
                noabove := noabove + 1
            else
                nobelow := nobelow + 1;

        read(length)
    until length < 0;

    writeln(nowithin, ' values are within tolerance.');
    writeln(noabove,  ' values are too large.');
    writeln(nobelow,  ' values are too small.')
end.
```

We finish this section by drawing your attention to a minor
difficulty which can arise when nesting if-statements, some of
which have no else-part. The computer always assumes that an else
belongs to the nearest unterminated if...then. Thus in a statement
such as

```
if  condition1  then
    if  condition2  then  statementa
    else  statementb
```

the else belongs to the second if and the computer will behave  as

94

follows:

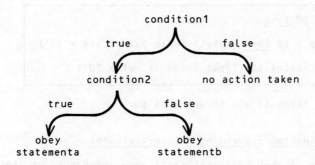

For example, when the computer obeys the statement

```
if x > 50 then
    if y > 50 then writeln('both values > 50')
    else writeln('only the first value is > 50')
```

no action at all is taken if x <= 50.

If necessary, begin...end brackets can be used to terminate an if...then as follows:

```
if  condition1  then
begin
    if  condition2  then  statementa
end
else statementb
```

The begin...end indicate that the enclosed if-then-statement is complete and the following else is taken as belonging to the first if. In this case the computer behaves as follows:

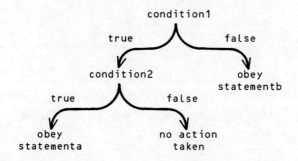

For example, if the computer obeys the statement:

```
if x > 50 then
begin
    if y > 50 then writeln('both values are > 50')
end
else writeln('the first value is not > 50')
```

no action is taken if x > 50 and y <= 50.

## 6.4 Data validation - guarding a case-statement

In Chapter 4 when case-statements were introduced we mentioned that if the selector did not contain one of the labels in the case-statement, the program would fail. This is obviously undesirable and in PASCAL it is the programmer's responsibility to guard against such an eventuality. In practice this means that a case-statement may have to be protected by a structure which ensures that the case-statement is not obeyed unless the value of the selector does correspond to one of the labels:

```
if   selector has a sensible value  then

    case-statement

else   write an error message
```

The next program uses this structure.

### Program 6.9
This is a program which is to control a "coin in the slot" machine. We assume that coins of denomination 50, 10, 5, 2, and 1 have weights of 35, 16, 9, 7 and 3 respectively. Also we are simulating a single coin being put in th slot by "read(weight)". The program is to print a message as soon as at least £1.23 has been inserted, calculating any change due.

96

```
program coins(input,output);

var weight : integer;
    total : real;

begin
    total := 0;

    repeat
        read(weight);

        if weight in [35,16,9,7,3] then

            case weight of
                35 : total := total + 50;
                16 : total := total + 10;
                 9 : total := total +  5;
                 7 : total := total +  2;
                 3 : total := total +  1
            end

        else writeln('coin rejected')

    until total >= 123;

    write('coins accepted.');
    if total > 123 then
        writeln(' change due: ', total - 123)
end.
```

In the above program, we have introduced the operator in which
can be used to test whether a value is one of a given set of
values. A test such as

(weight = 35) or (weight = 16) or (weight) = 9) or
(weight = 7 ) or (weight = 3 )

is rather cumbersome. This condition is more concisely expressed
as

weight in [35, 16, 9, 7, 3]

We can test whether a given integer is in the range 1 to 10 by
using a condition such as

(1 <= i) and (i <= 10)

but this can also be more concisely expressed in set notation as

i in [1..10]

The elements of a set in the above sense can not be real numbers
and you may find that your PASCAL system imposes some further
restrictions on the range of values which can appear in a set
(inside the square brackets). This is a consequence of the way
such a set is represented inside the computer.

## 6.5 Data validation - guarding a program

When it is possible to check or validate the data input to a program this should always be done. Not only does this guard against the possibility of an execution error, the cause of which might not be immediately apparent, but worse - invalid data may cause erroneous results which go unnoticed. In simple cases, we can use a structure such as:

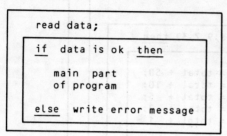

```
read data;

if data is ok then

    main part
    of program

else  write error message
```

The following program uses this structure. The individual case-statements do not need guarding because in each the selector has already been checked.

### Program 6.10

This program calculates the cost of a holiday by multiplying the duration in days by a daily rate which is seasonally dependant. The input data is two dates in the form day, month and we assume that the months are either going to be identical or consecutive. Also we assume that it is the second month which determines the seasonal rate.

```
program holiday(input,output);

const lowrate = 57;
      midrate = 72;
      peakrate= 87;
var day1, month1, day2, month2, duration,
    tillendofmonth, cost : integer;

begin
    read(day1,month1,day2,month2);

    if (day1 in [1..31]) and (day2 in [1..31])
        and (month1 in [1..12]) and (month2 in [1..12])
        and (month1 <= month2)   then

    begin
        if month1 = month2 then
            duration := day2 - day1 +1
        else
        begin
            case month1 of
                      2 : tillendofmonth := 28 - day1;
              9,4,6,11 : tillendofmonth := 30 - day1;
              1,3,5,7,
              8,10,12 : tillendofmonth := 31 - day1
            end;
            duration := day2 + tillendofmonth + 1
        end;

        case month2 of
        1,2,11,12 : cost := duration*lowrate;
        3,4,5,10  : cost := duration*midrate;
        6,7,8,9   : cost := duration*peakrate
        end;

        write('cost of holiday is ', cost)
    end
    else write('you have typed erroneous dates')

end.
```

In this example we have simplified the input data check (not every
month has 31 days!); but comprehensive validation would be too
lengthy for the purpose of this demonstration.

The innermost box is entered only if the data is acceptable
(within the limits of the test used). If the data is erroneous the
computer will have to be told to execute the program again. If a
program is required to automatically request more input until a
correct set of data values have typed, then the following
structure can be used:

```
read data;

while data is faulty do
begin
   write a message requesting data to be retyped;
   read data
end;

┌─────────────┐
│ main  part  │
│ of program  │
└─────────────┘
```

In the case of program 6.10, use of this structure would give us:

```
read(day1,month1,day2,month2);

while not ( (day1 in [1..31]) and (day2 in [1..31])
        and (month1 in [1..12]) and (month2 in [1..12])
        and (month1 <= month2) )  do
begin
   write('you have made an error please retype');
   read(day1,month1,day2,month2)
end;

┌──────────────────────────────────┐
│ calculation part of program      │
└──────────────────────────────────┘
```

## 6.6 Stepwise refinement

In writing some of the programs in this chapter, we have
informally introduced the technique that is sometimes termed
**stepwise refinement** or **top-down program design.** Instead of
attempting to write down a complete PASCAL program in one step, we
first decide what the outermost control structure in the program
should be. For example, in writing Program 6.6, we can see
immediately that there are 63 separate sales analyses to be made.
Giving a brief English description to the process of analyzing one
department's sales enabled us to write down an outline of this
loop:

```
for dept := 1 to 63 do
   ┌──────────────────────────────────┐
   │ analyze the sales for one department │
   └──────────────────────────────────┘
```

Having got this clear in our minds, we then concentrated on the
rather easier sub-problem of analyzing one department's sales and
the program for doing this was eventually inserted in the above
structure. This sub-problem was of course tackled by a further
application of stepwise refinement.

100

Such an approach enables the construction of a complex nested control structure to be broken down into a number of simpler programming tasks that are more or less independent of each other. This is just one aspect of the set of programming techniques known as **structured programming.**

Stepwise refinement is discussed further in Chapter 9.

Exercises for Chapter 6

1) Given input data consisting of 30 numbers, some of which are positive and some of which are negative, write a program which finds the average of the positive numbers and the average of the negative numbers.

2) Write a program that accepts as input a set of sample diameter readings from one of the ball-bearing machines described in Exercise 7, Chapter 5. A ball-bearing is classified as faulty if its diameter is less than 1.99mm or greater than 2.01 mm. Your program should report the percentage of faulty ball-bearings in the sample.

   Now extend your program to accept two successive sets of readings from two machines and to report which machine is producing the smaller proportion of faulty samples.

3) Write a program which accepts as input data 2 numbers representing the width and height of a rectangle. The program is then to print such a rectangle made up of asterisks, for example:

   ```
   ******
   ******
   ******
   ```

4) Write a program to accept a single integer and print a multipication table for all the positive integers up to the one specified as input.

5) Write a program that will read the lengths of three sides of a triangle (three integers) and which will print the lengths of the sides in descending order followed by a message to say whether the triangle is right-angled.

6) Extend your solution to Exercise 5 to include a test to check that the data does in fact specify a legal triangle. (The sum of the two smallest sides must be greater than the largest side.)

7) The monthly life insurance premium charged by an insurance company is dependent on the age of the applicant. A basic premium of $5 is charged but this may be subject to one or more $2 increments. Only applicants who will not be 65 or over on their next birthday are eligible and the number of

increments is determined by the applicant's age as follows:

| age next birthday | increments |
|---|---|
| < 20 | 0 |
| >= 21 and < 30 | 1 |
| >= 30 and < 45 | 2 |
| >= 45 and < 65 | 3 |

Write a program to print the monthly premium for an applicant. The data input is date-of-birth and current-date each as three integers.

8) Write a program that accepts as input the numbers of two months (in the same year) followed by the number of the year, and outputs the total number of days from the beginning of the first month to the end of the second month.

9) Extend your solution to Exercise 8 so that it accepts two dates in the form, for example:

13  6
25  12

where the first number in each pair is a day and the second is a month. Again assume that both dates are in the same year. The dates will be followed in the input by the number of the year. The program should print the number of days from the first date to the second date.

# 7 Working with characters

Hitherto, characters typed as input to our programs have been numeric characters grouped together to represent numbers in the usual way. Many computer applications involve handling non-numeric data. For example, an organization may want to use a computer program to process a list of its customer's names and addresses; a telephone customer account number might be a combination of letters and digits which has to be handled by a computer program; a student of literature might use a computer program to analyze a piece of text that he is studying. PASCAL programs usually have to store and process such non-numeric data one character at a time.

## 7.1 Character variables and character input

In this section we shall introduce some PASCAL facilities which will enable us to write programs that manipulate the individual characters supplied as input to a program.

Program 7.1
This program reads three characters and writes these three characters in reverse order.

```
program reverse(input,output);

var first, second, third : char;

begin
    read(first, second, third);
    writeln(third, second, first)
end.
```

In addition to the types "integer", "real" and "boolean" we now have the type "char". "first", "second" and "third" are variables in each of which a single character can be stored. If this program is supplied with input:

bat

then after obeying the read statement, the character variables contain:

first  'b'        second  'a'        third  't'

103

As in the case of strings, character values are always written in quotation marks to avoid confusion with the names of variables. On this occasion, the write-statement has the same effect as

```
write('t', 'a', 'b')
```

and output thus consists of

tab

Input of

*-+

results in output of

+-*

Input of

467

results in output of

764

In this last case, you should note that, although the three characters in the input could be treated as making up a single number, this program reads and stores the input as three separate digits, each being stored in a separate character variable.

Frequently a program for manipulating characters has to distinguish one group of characters from another. For example, a program manipulating the words in a piece of text may have to treat the punctuation characters between words differently from the letters constituting the words. In other cases, a program may be required to distinguish separate lines of input.

Program 7.2
This program ignores any spaces that may be typed at the start of
the input, and then prints all permutations of the three
characters that follow.

```
program anagrams(input,output);

var first, second, third : char;

begin
   repeat
      read(first)
   until first <> ' ';

   read(second, third);

   writeln(first,second,third, ' ', first,third,second);
   writeln(second,first,third, ' ', second,third,first);
   writeln(third,first,second, ' ', third,second,first)
end.
```

Given input of

        cat

(preceded by any number of spaces), this program produces output

cat    cta
act    atc
tca    tac


   When input for a program is being typed at a keyboard, a
special end-of-line key is pressed to mark the end of a line. For
example, on many computers the RETURN key is used for this
purpose. Pressing this key inserts an "end-of-line marker" in the
input. In order that input to a program can be processed on a
line-by-line basis, a special function "eoln" is available.
("eoln" stands for "end of line".) This function has a boolean
result and can be used to detect that the next unread character in
the input is the end-of-line marker. Thus a program can count how
many characters were typed on a line before the end-of-line key
was pressed:

```
var nextchar : char;  count : integer;
   .
   .
   count := 0;
   while not eoln(input) do
   begin
      read(nextchar);
      count := count + 1
   end
```

105

Here, we have used a while-statement in case the input line happens to be blank. Note that the "eoln" function does not remove the end-of-line marker from the input and "eoln" will still have the value "true" after the above loop has terminated.

The official definition of the PASCAL language permits the parameter "input" and the surrounding brackets to be omitted after "eoln". However, a parameter is needed in more advanced applications and some PASCAL systems require that the parameter should always be supplied. In this book we always include the parameter.

When the end-of-line marker is actually read by a PASCAL program, it is treated as a space. Consider the following program fragment:

```
var ch1, ch2, ch3, ch4 : char;
   .
   .
   .
read(ch1, ch2, ch3, ch4);
write(ch1, ch2, ch3, ch4)
```

If the read statement is supplied with input

abcd

the write-statement will print

abcd

Given input of

ab
c

where the end-of-line key is pressed immediately after the 'b', output will be

ab c

Pressing the end-of-line key after the 'b' has in effect inserted an extra space in the input. Consider the fragment:

```
count := 0;
repeat
   read(ch1);
   count := count + 1
until ch1 = 'z';
writeln(count, 'characters were read.')
```

Let the input be

```
abcdef
ghijklmn
opqrstu
vwxy
z
```

where the end-of-line key is pressed immediately after the last letter on each line. The output will be

30 characters were read.

where the 30 characters are made up of 26 letters and 4 end-of-line markers (spaces).

Finally, we again draw your attention to the distinction between a character and the name of a variable. Consider:

```
var a : char;
  .
  .
  .
  read(a);
  writeln(a, 'a')
```

The writeln statement will print **the contents of the variable called** "a" followed by the character **'a'**.

| input | output |
|-------|--------|
| z     | za     |
| *     | *a     |
| a     | aa     |

## 7.2 Files

The string of characters supplied as input to a program is usually referred to as a **file.** We have already mentioned (Section 5.1) the possibility of a program reading its input from a file stored on a magnetic disk or tape. From now onwards, we will sometimes assume that the input to a program is provided in this way. This will make it possible to write programs which process realistically large input files without a large file having to be typed at the keyboard each time a program is tested. It will also avoid the possibility of a program's input and output becoming mixed up on the same piece of paper or on the screen attached to our keyboard. The way a file is originally typed onto disk or tape will depend on the computing system you are using. We shall assume that there is some facility for telling the computer that a program should take its input from a particular stored file when it is executed. For example, to obey a program, you may have to type something like:

```
execute anagrams, input=wordfile
```

where "wordfile" is the name that has been given to a file of characters which has been typed onto disk.

When a previously typed file is to be used as input by a program, the function "eof" can be used to detect when the end of the input file has been reached. This can happen only immediately after an end-of-line marker. "eof" stands for "end of file". For example, the following fragment of program will count how many characters (including end-of-line markers) there are in a given input file:

```
count := 0;
repeat
    read(nextchar);  count := count + 1
until eof(input);
writeln('there are ', count, ' characters in the file.')
```

Program 7.3
This program counts the number of occurrences of a given character in a piece of text supplied in an input file. The given character is specified as a named constant.

```
program charcount(input,output);

const givench = 'e';

var noofoccurrences : integer;  nextch : char;

begin
    noofoccurrences := 0;
    repeat
        read(nextch);
        if nextch = givench then
            noofoccurrences := noofoccurrences + 1
    until eof(input);
    writeln('the character ', givench, ' appears ',
            noofoccurrences, ' times.')
end.
```

As with "eoln", the parameter "input" and the surrounding brackets could be omitted.

108

## 7.3 Character ordering

When we are handling numbers, we can ask if one number comes before or after another number by using expressions such as "x < y", "count >= 3", "r <= 23.47", and so on. We are able to do this because there is a natural ordering defined for the integers and real numbers. In fact there is also an ordering defined for the characters that can be handled by a PASCAL program. Characters can be compared using the operators "<", ">", "<=" and ">=". You will find in particular that:

      'a' is before 'b' with no other character in between.
      'b' is before 'c' with no other character in between.
      'c' is before 'd' with no other character in between.
       .         .
       .         .
       .         .
      'y' is before 'z' with no other character in between.

      and

      '0' is before '1' with no other character in between.
      '1' is before '2' with no other character in between.
       .         .
       .         .
       .         .
      '8' is before '9' with no other character in between.

We can therefore test whether the character in the variable "ch" is alphabetic by using the expression

    (ch >= 'a') and (ch <= 'z')

or, more neatly, by

    ch in ['a'..'z']

We can test whether a character is a numeric digit by using the expression

    (ch >= '0') and (ch <= '9')

or again by

    ch in ['0' ..'9']

In general, we shall probably not be interested in whether a character such as '*' comes before or after a character such as '='. In fact, the position of such non-alphanumeric characters in the ordering will vary from one PASCAL system to another.

Program 7.4
This reads one character and prints a message indicating whether it is alphabetic, numeric or otherwise.

```
program classifychar(input,output);

var character : char;

begin
    read(character);
    if character in ['a'..'z'] then
        writeln('that character is alphabetic.')
    else if character in ['0'..'9'] then
            writeln('that character is numeric.')
        else
            writeln('that character is not alphanumeric.')
end.
```

Program 7.5
This program reads a word and counts how many letters it contains. Any non-alphabetic characters before the word are ignored and the last letter of the word is followed in the input by a non-alphabetic character.

```
program wordlength(input,output);

var nextchar : char;  noofletters : integer;

begin
    repeat
        read(nextchar)
    until nextchar in ['a'..'z'];
(* at this point, nextchar will contain the first
                            letter of the word *)
    noofletters := 0;
    repeat
        noofletters := noofletters + 1;
        read(nextchar)
    until not (nextchar in ['a'..'z']);
(* at this point, nextchar will contain the first
                        character after the word *)
    writeln('no. of letters: ', noofletters)
end.
```

Program 7.6
Given a piece of text, this program counts the percentage of the letters in the text that are equal to a given letter.

```
program letterfrequ(input,output);

const givenletter = 'e';

var noofletters, noofgivenletter : integer;
    character : char;

begin
    noofletters := 0;  noofgivenletter := 0;
    repeat
        read(character);
        if character in ['a'..'z'] then
        begin
            noofletters := noofletters + 1;
            if character = givenletter then
                noofgivenletter := noofgivenletter + 1
        end
    until eof(input);
    writeln(noofgivenletter/noofletters*100,
            '% of the letters were ', givenletter, '-s.')
end.
```

Output produced by the above program might be

16.54% of the letters were e-s.

   The following program illustrates how a piece of text can be processed on a word-by-word basis. It counts the total number of words in a sentence and counts the number of four-letter words in the same sentence. We assume for simplicity that the sentence is terminated by a full stop typed immediately after the last word. We can summarize what we want this program to do as follows:

```
noofwords := 0; noof4words := 0;
repeat
    find start of next word;
    read next word and count letters in it;
    noofwords := noofwords + 1;
    if noofletters = 4 then noof4words := noof4words + 1
until nextchar ='.'
```

Finding the start of a word and then counting the letters in the word involves obeying two separate loops one after the other as in Program 7.5, but in this case the section of program containing these loops must be obeyed once for each word in the sentence as outlined above. We thus require a construction involving an outer repeat-statement which contains a sequence of two inner repeat-statements. We shall arrange that after the start of a word has

been found, "nextchar" contains the first character of the word
and, after a word has been read, "nextchar" contains the first
character after the word. The complete program is given below.

Program 7.7

```
program countwords(input, output);

var nextch : char;
    noofletters, noofwords, noof4words : integer;

begin
    noofwords := 0; noof4words := 0;

    repeat

        repeat read(nextch) until nextch in ['a'..'z'];

        noofletters := 0;
        repeat
            noofletters := noofletters + 1;
            read(nextch)
        until not (nextch in ['a'..'z']);

        noofwords := noofwords + 1;
        if noofletters = 4 then noof4words := noof4words + 1
    until nextch ='.';

    writeln('words in sentence: ', noofwords);
    writeln('4-letter words in sentence: ', noof4words)
end.
```

Because of the ordering defined for the characters, we can use
a character variable as the control variable in a for-statement:

```
var letter : char;
    .
    .
    .
    for letter := 'a' to 'z' do
        write(letter)
```

will print

abcdefghijklmnopqrstuvwxyz

The statement

```
for letter := 'z' downto 'a' do
    write(letter)
```

will print

zyxwvutsrqponmlkjihgfedcba


## 7.4 Further facilities for character manipulation

The function "pred" can be used to obtain the character that comes immediately before a given character in the ordering - its "predecessor". For example

```
writeln(pred('b'), 'b')
```

will print

ab

Similarly, "succ" is used to obtain the "successor" of a given character.

```
ch := 'j';
writeln(pred(ch), ch, succ(ch))
```

will print

ijk

## Program 7.8
A message is to be coded by replacing each letter in the message by the succeeding letter in the alphabet, 'z' being replaced by 'a'. This program reads a piece of text from a file and prints the message in its coded form. The line by line structure of the original message is maintained.

```
program code(input,output);

var character : char;

begin

   repeat

      while not eoln(input) do
      begin
         read(character);
         if character in ['a'..'z'] then
            if character = 'z' then write('a')
            else write(succ(character))
         else write(character);
      end;

      readln;  writeln
   until eof(input)

end.
```

The internal loop in the above program encodes a single line of
text. A while-statement is used in order to cover the possibility
that a line may be blank. At the end of each line of input, the
program uses "readln" to to find the start of the next line of
input and it uses "writeln" to start a new line of output.

Each character which can be handled in a PASCAL system has an
"ordinal number" (an integer) associated with it. A character's
ordinal number is determined by the position of the character in
the overall character ordering. The first character has ordinal
number 0, the next has ordinal number 1 and so on. The function
"ord" converts a character into its ordinal number, and the
function "chr" converts an integer into the character with that
ordinal number. The character ordering, and hence the ordinal
numbers associated with the characters, will vary from one PASCAL
system to another. You could find out what the ordinal numbers are
on your system by obeying:

```
var ordinal : integer;
        .
        .
   for ordinal := 0 to 63 do
      writeln('character ', chr(ordinal),
              ' has ordinal number ', ordinal)
```

There may in fact be more than 64 characters in your system. The
ordinal numbers associated with the alphabetic characters could be
printed by using:

```
var ch : char;
   .
   .
   for ch := 'a' to 'z' do
      writeln(ch, ' ', ord(ch))
```

In general, you do not need to know what the ordinal numbers are, so long as you remember that, for example, the alphabetic characters have consecutive ordinal numbers. We could print the "n"th letter of the alphabet by using:

```
var n : integer;
   .
   .
   read(n);
   write('letter ', n, ' is ', chr(ord('a') + n - 1))
```

Program 7.9
This program codes a message as in Program 7.8. In this case, each letter in the message is replaced by the letter a given number of places ahead in the alphabet. This given number is defined as a named constant. As before, the alphabet is to be treated as circular, 'a' being assumed to follow 'z'.

```
program codeshift(input,output);

const shift = 5;

var character : char;  ordinal : integer;

begin

   repeat

      while not eoln(input) do
      begin
         read(character);
         if character in ['a'..'z'] then
         begin
            ordinal := ord(character);
            ordinal := ordinal + shift;
            if ordinal > ord('z') then
               ordinal := ordinal - 26;
            write(chr(ordinal))
         end
         else write(character)
      end;

      readln;  writeln
   until eof(input)

end.
```

115

Finally, we present a facility which enables a program to examine the next character in the input without actually reading and storing it. The expression "input↑" has as its value the next character in the input file. A full explanation of the use of the symbol "↑" is beyond the scope of this book, but for handling character input it is occasionally useful. In the following program we also introduce the procedure "get" which can be used to "read and ignore" the next character in the input.

Program 7.10
This program reads an integer which tells it how many further integers are to be read and added together. The integers in the input may be interspersed with extraneous text which must be ignored by the program. For example, the input might be

on our street 4 different professions are represented:
there are 11 doctors, 16 dentists,
5 engineers and 103 civil servants.
how many professionals are there?

```
program addup(input,output);

var noofintegers, count, next, total : integer;

begin

    while not (input↑ in ['0'..'9']) do
        get(input);
    read(noofintegers);


    total := 0;
    for count := 1 to noofintegers do
    begin
        while not (input↑ in ['0'..'9']) do
            get(input);
        read(next);
        total := total + next
    end;


    while input↑ <> '?' do get(input);

    get(input);  (* remove question mark *)

    writeln('total is ', total)
end.
```

Given the input illustrated above, this program outputs

total is 135

The first boxed section of the program finds and reads the first integer in the data. When the read-statement is obeyed, the first digit of the integer has not yet been removed from the input, and is still available to be processed by the read-statement. The third boxed section of the program does not serve any useful purpose as the program stands. However, we might later want to extend the program to deal with further input of some sort. This section of the program simply ensures that the program reads all characters associated with the data which has been processed so far.

There are a number of important application areas in which character processing programs are used. In subsequent chapters, some of the examples will introduce programming techniques involved in areas such as word processing, textual analysis, and programming-language translation.

## Exercises for chapter 7

1) Write a program which will read a word of four letters. The word is to be printed again by the program, except that if it is the same as a given word (specified by means of four named character constants), it should be censored, the middle two characters being replaced by asterisks.

2) Write a program which will read a file of text and which will print a message indicating the total number of alphabetic characters in the text and another message indicating the total number of non-alphabetic characters (including end-of-line markers).

3) The input file for a program consists of a list of names, one name to a line. Each name consists of two forenames followed by a surname. The two forenames and the surname are separated from each other by one space, for example

   james jardine mcgregor
   john stuart smith
   alan henry watt
   .
   .
   .

   Write a program which reads such a file and prints each name in the form of a surname followed by two initials, for example:

   mcgregor, j.j.
   smith, j.s.
   watt, a.h.
   .
   .
   .

4) Each line in a file contains a distance in miles (an integer)

followed by the name of a town which lies at that distance from London. Write a program which will read this file and print a list of the names of towns which are less than 100 miles from London.

5) A message is decoded by replacing each letter in the message by the letter n steps ahead in the alphabet. The alphabet is considered to be circular and 'a' is treated as being one step ahead of 'z'. Write a program which will print a table for use in the manual coding and decoding of messages for a given value of n. For example, with n=4, the table would be:

```
letter:        abcdefghijklmnopqrstuvwxyz
coded letter:  efghijklmnopqrstuvwxyzabcd
```

6) A file contains information about a company's salaried employees. Each line of the file contains the name of an employee (made up to exactly 25 characters by inserting extra spaces if necessary), followed by his annual salary in pounds. Write a program which will print a monthly payslip for each employee in the file. Assume that each annual salary can be divided by 12 without involving fractions of a penny and that tax is deducted at a flat rate of 30%.

7) Write a program which counts how many words there are in a sentence and also counts how many of these words begin with the letter 'a'. The last word in the sentence is followed immediately by a full stop.

8) A music shop has done a stock-taking of all the musical instruments in stock. The list is to be input to a computer program in the form, for example:

```
3 violins,  2 cellos.
1 french horn, 2 trumpets and 3 cornets;
etc.
```

where the punctuation is arbitrary. Assume that each instrument is mentioned only once in the list. Write a program which ignores the non-numeric characters and reports the number of different instruments in stock (the number of numerical entries in the file) as well as the total number of instruments in stock.

9) Write a program which reads a piece of text and checks that it obeys the spelling rule: 'i' comes before 'e' except after 'c'.

# 8 Handling collections of values: arrays

If a program systematically processes a collection of variables, it may not be convenient for the programmer to give each of these variables a different name. For example it would be rather tedious to write:

```
totalprice := priceofhammer + priceofsaw    +
              priceofaxe    + priceofplane  +
              priceofchisel + priceofvice   +
              priceofscrewd + priceofspanner;
```

Instead of giving such a group of variables separate names, it is often more convenient to give them a collective name and to refer to the individual variables in the collection by subscripts, where the subscripts may be numbers.

## 8.1 One-dimensional arrays

A one-dimensional array is a set of storage locations or variables all of the same type which share the same name, but have different subscripts. For example the information:

| name of variable | content |
|---|---|
| priceofhammer | 5.77 |
| priceofsaw | 3.15 |
| priceofaxe | 2.50 |
| priceofplane | 16.33 |
| priceofchisel | 2.50 |
| priceofvice | 13.45 |
| priceofscrewd | .86 |
| priceofspanner | 1.98 |

could be stored in a one-dimensional array:

```
name of variable         content
     priceof[1]            5.77
     priceof[2]            3.15
     priceof[3]            2.50
     priceof[4]           16.33
     priceof[5]            2.50
     priceof[6]           13.45
     priceof[7]            .86
     priceof[8]           1.98
```

The numbers in square brackets are the distinguishing subscripts.
Arrays have to be declared, and for our example the declarations
could be:

```
var  priceof : array [1..8] of real;
```

In this declaration "priceof" is the name of the array. The
numbers in square brackets are the least and greatest subscripts
separated by two dots. "of real" means that the variables are to
contain reals. In a program, the subscript used to select a
location of the above array can be an integer constant, an integer
variable, or indeed any integer expression as long as the value of
the subscript is in the range 1..8. This has the advantage that we
can use a loop to systematically process all the values in the
array (a point we shall return to later). For example:

```
totalprice := 0;
for itemno := 1 to 8 do
    totalprice := totalprice + priceof[itemno]
```

The variables that make up an array are called array elements.
Array elements can be manipulated just like simple variables. For
example:

```
read(price[1], price[2], price[3], price[4]);
read(price[5], price[6], price[7], price[8]);
writeln('the price of item 2 is ',price[2]);
writeln('the price of item 4 is ',price[4]);

writeln('the price difference between items 1 and 2 is ',
        abs(price[1] - price[2]));

difference := price[1] - price[2];
if difference > 0 then
    writeln('item 1 costs ', difference,
            ' more than item 2.')
else  if difference < 0 then
         writeln('item 2 costs ', -difference,
                 ' more than item 1.')
```

## 8.2 Sequential access to one-dimensional arrays

In the following example we have declared an array of ten integer locations all named "number".

## Program 8.1
This program reads ten integers and prints them in reverse order.

```
program reverse(input,output);

var number : array [1..10] of integer;
    position : integer;

begin

    for position := 1 to 10 do
        read(number[position]);

    for position := 10 downto 1 do
        writeln(number[position])

end.
```

In Program 8.1 the array elements are accessed systematically one after another. This is a very simple example of sequential access. The program reads input integers into successive locations. It then starts at the tenth location and fetches the integers in reverse order printing them as it goes. A control structure appropriate for these actions is a for-statement and we use the control variable "position" as an array subscript. The execution of the first for-statement proceeds as follows:

| value of "position" | statement obeyed |
|---|---|
| 1 | read(number[1]) |
| 2 | read(number[2]) |
| 3 | read(number[3]) |
| . | . |
| . | . |
| . | . |

It is important to note that each array location has two quantities associated with it:

1) the subscript,
2) the contents of the location.

## Program 8.2

Given a price list containing four prices, and a list of four numbers indicating the quantity purchased of each of the four items, the program calculates the total price. (The "priceof" table is initialized by a list of assignment statements. This may seem somewhat tedious but it simulates a more realistic situation where the table would be initialized by reading prices from a file.)

```pascal
program prices(input,output);

var priceof : array [1..4] of real;
    itemno, quantity : integer;
    total : real;

begin

    priceof[1] := 5.77;
    priceof[2] := 3.15;
    priceof[3] := 2.50;
    priceof[4] := 1.35;

    total := 0;

    for itemno := 1 to 4 do
    begin
        read(quantity);
        total := total + quantity*priceof[itemno]
    end;

    writeln('the total cost is ',total)
end.
```

In Program 8.1 we used an array of integers and in Program 8.2 an array of reals. The next program uses an array of characters.

Program 8.3
Reads an integer "n" followed on the next line by an "n" letter
word, and prints the word backwards.

```
program word(input,output);

var letter : array [1..20] of char;
    n, i : integer;

begin

    readln(n);
    for i := 1 to n do
        read(letter[i]);

    writeln;
    for i := n downto 1 do
        write(letter[i])

end.
```

In the above program, the readln statement reads the integer and
then finds the start of the next line of input, so that that the
next character read will be the first character of the word.

    When an array element is referred to in a program, the value of
the subscript must always be within the subscript range that has
been declared. Let us consider what would have happened in Program
8.2 if we had typed:

```
for itemno := 1 to 5 do
```

At one stage, the computer would attempt to refer to "priceof[5]"
which does not exist and the program would fail during execution.
If the program is required to store 5 prices, the array should be
declared as:

```
var priceof : array[1..5] of real;
```

    Now look at Program 8.3. Here the value of "n" is specified
from the keyboard while the program is running. If we type in a
number greater than 20 then the program will fail when it attempts
to store something in "letter[21]". We could guard against this
eventuality by checking the input value, as suggested in Chapter
6. Note also that if "n" is less than 20, only part of the array
is used.

## 8.3 Random access to a one-dimensional array

The following program illustrates the use of an array where the elements are being accessed randomly rather than in a sequential manner.

### Program 8.4
Given two item numbers in the range 1-4 the program prints the corresponding prices.

```
program prices2(input,output);

var priceof : array [1..4] of real;
    itema, itemb : integer;

begin

    priceof[1] := 5.77;
    priceof[2] := 3.15;
    priceof[3] := 2.50;
    priceof[4] := 1.35;

    read(itema, itemb);
    writeln('item no. ', itema, ' costs ', priceof[itema]);
    writeln('item no. ', itemb, ' costs ', priceof[itemb])

end.
```

In this program the two elements are not accessed in any particular order. When the program is executed, we could type 3 followed by 1. The program would then access "priceof[3]" followed by "priceof[1]". We say that the array has been accessed randomly. The process can be illustrated diagramatically as:

The two numbers typed from the keyboard are placed in the integer variables "itema" and "itemb". The contents of "itema" are used to select one of the 4 elements of "price". The process is then repeated for "itemb". In this case, output would be:

item no. 3 costs 2.50
item no. 1 costs 5.77

In this case, if a number other than 1,2,3 or 4 had been typed as input, the program would have failed.

The next two programs use a mixture of sequential and random access.

## Program 8.5

Six candidates in an election have reference numbers 1,2,3,...6. A list of votes (terminated by -1) takes the form of a list of such reference numbers For example:

number typed

```
    5          means 1 vote for candidate 5
    3          means 1 vote for candidate 3
    1          means 1 vote for candidate 1
    3          means 1 more vote for candidate 3
    .
    .
   -1          means "end of list"
```

The program totalizes the votes for each candidate and finds the winner.

```
program votes(input,output);

var candidate, mostvotesofar, winner : integer;
    votesfor : array [1..6] of integer;

begin

    for candidate := 1 to 6 do
        votesfor[candidate] := 0;


    read(candidate);
    repeat
        votesfor[candidate] := votesfor[candidate] + 1;
        read(candidate);
    until candidate = -1;


    mostvotesofar := 0;
    for candidate := 1 to 6 do
        if votesfor[candidate] > mostvotesofar then
            begin
                mostvotesofar := votesfor[candidate];
                winner := candidate
            end;

    writeln('winner is candidate no. ',winner);
end.
```

125

In the first box the 6 elements of "votesfor" are initialized to zero using sequential access. In the second box each number typed in from the list determines which of the 6 elements is to be incremented - random access. The third box finds the element that now contains the highest integer.

Program 8.6
Reads 2 dates each in the form day, month, and calculates the number of days from one day to the next. It is assumed that the dates are sensible and that they lie in the same year which is not a leap year. (This program illustrates an alternative method of solution, using an array, for Exercise 9, Chapter 6.)

```
program days(input,output);

var month, daystogo, firstday,
    firstmonth, secondday, secondmonth : integer;
    daysin : array [1..12] of integer;

begin
  for month := 1 to 12 do

    case month of
                  2: daysin[month] := 28;
          9,4,6,11: daysin[month] := 30;
    1,3,5,7,8,10,12: daysin[month] := 31
    end;

  read(firstday,firstmonth,secondday,secondmonth);
  if firstmonth = secondmonth then
    daystogo := secondday - firstday
  else
  begin

    daystogo := daysin[firstmonth] - firstday;

    for month := firstmonth + 1 to secondmonth - 1 do
    daystogo := daystogo + daysin[month];

    daystogo := daystogo + secondday

  end;

  writeln('days to go:', daystogo)

end.
```

In this program the initialization of "daysin" is achieved by a case-statement inside a for-statement. The for-statement controls the sequential access and the case-statement selects the appropriate value for each element. If the two days are not in the same month then the program calculates the number of days to go by

adding 3 fragments (3 boxes above) to "daystogo". For example if
the input was:

```
 5    2
20    5
```

the program would select the appropriate numbers as follows:

daysin

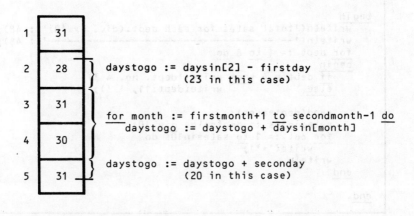

```
daystogo := daysin[2] - firstday
            (23 in this case)

for month := firstmonth+1 to secondmonth-1 do
     daystogo := daystogo + daysin[month]

daystogo := daystogo + seconday
            (20 in this case)
```

## 8.4 Drawing histograms

The following histogram was produced by a daily sales  analysis
program.

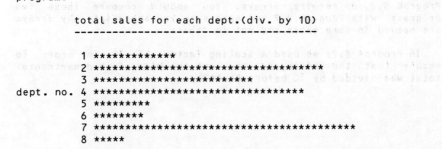

```
          total sales for each dept.(div. by 10)
          -------------------------------------------
          1 *************
          2 ************************************
          3 *************************
dept. no. 4 *********************************
          5 *********
          6 ********
          7 *****************************************
          8 *****
```

The **length** of each line indicates visually the total sales in each
of eight departments and is easier and quicker to interpret than a
list of eight numbers. The total sales for each department is
approximately indicated by the number of stars on each line
multiplied by 10. We are constraining the histogram to a
reasonable width by counting each department's sales in tens. The
next program illustrates techniques used in drawing such diagrams.

Program 8.7
Prints a histogram, given, in an input file, a list of eight
numbers representing the daily sales total for each of eight
departments. (We assume that dividing each number by 10 gives a
display of suitable width.)

```
program salesanalysis2(input,output);

var dept, col, deptsales, salesin10s : integer;

begin
    writeln('total sales for each dept.(div. by 10)' : 48);
    writeln('----------------------------------------' : 48);
    for dept := 1 to 8 do
    begin
        if dept = 4 then write('dept. no. 4 ')
        else                write(dept:11, ' ');

        read(deptsales);
        salesin10s := deptsales div 10;
        for col := 1 to salesin10s do
            write('*');
        writeln
    end

end.
```

Note that Program 8.7 does not use an array - there is no need to
store any of the departmental sales for subsequent reference. It
is a common error among new programmers to use arrays
unnecessarily. Programs 8.8 and 8.9, simple elaborations of
Program 8.7, do require arrays. You should compare these two
programs with Program 8.7 and make sure you appreciate why arrays
are needed in some cases and not in others.

In Program 8.7, we used a **scaling factor** of 10 in order to
ensure that the histogram was not too wide. Each departmental
total was divided by 10 before plotting.

128

Program 8.8
As Program 8.7 except that the program is to determine a suitable scaling factor. We assume a line width of 60 and that the maximum sales total is much greater than this.

```
program salesanlaysis3(input,output);

const lengthofline = 60;
var salesfor : array [1..8] of integer;
    dept, col, maxsofar, scaling, scaledtotal : integer;

begin
    maxsofar := 0;
    for dept := 1 to 8 do
    begin
        read(salesfor[dept]);
        if salesfor[dept] > maxsofar then
            maxsofar := salesfor[dept]
    end;

    scaling := 1 + maxsofar div lengthofline;

    for dept := 1 to 8 do
    begin
        write(dept, ' ');
        scaledtotal := salesfor[dept] div scaling;
        for col := 1 to scaledtotal do
            write('*');
        writeln
    end

end.
```

Program 8.9
As Program 8.7 except that the data is input as a long list of numbers, representing individual sales, terminated by -1. For example:

| number typed | |
|---|---|
| 5 | means 1 sale for dept. 5 |
| 3 | means 1 sale for dept. 3 |
| 1 | means 1 sale for dept. 1 |
| 3 | means 1 more sale for dept. 3 |
| . | . |
| . | . |
| . | . |
| -1 | means "end of list" |

Here we again use a scaling factor of 10.

```
program salesanalysis4(input,output);

var salesfor : array [1..8] of integer;
    dept, col, scaledtotal : integer;

begin
    for dept := 1 to 8 do
        salesfor[dept] := 0;

    read(dept);
    repeat
        salesfor[dept] := salesfor[dept] + 1;
        read(dept);
    until dept = -1;

    for dept := 1 to 8 do
    begin
        scaledtotal := salesfor[dept] div 10;
        for col := 1 to scaledtotal do
            write('*');
        writeln
    end;
end.
```

## 8.5 Two-dimensional arrays

Many techniques in science, engineering and commerce deal with data which is organized in two dimensions. Pictures from interplanetary explorers, for example, are enhanced and analyzed by computer. The pictures are represented inside the computer as a two-dimensional table of numbers. Each number corresponds to the brightness of a picture element or point. A picture is converted into a table of numbers by a special input device and after it is processed, it is converted back into a picture by a special output device. It is much easier and more natural for a programmer to think in terms of a two-dimensional set of picture elements - the picture retaining its two-dimensional form when referred to in the program - than it would be if the picture elements were strung out row-wise or column-wise into a one-dimensional array or list.

Consider another example - an 8x10 table of numbers (8 rows, 10 columns), where each number represents the population of the corresponding zone of an 8x10 square mile map. We can retain the two-dimensional nature of the data by storing it in a two-dimensional array "popmap". First of all let us see how we declare such an array.

```
var popmap : array [1..8,1..10] of integer;
```

This declaration has set up a two-dimensional structure of integer
variables into which we can place the data. It is usual to picture
a two-dimensional array as a collection of variables, all of the
same type, organized into rows and columns.

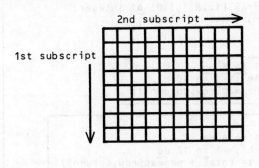

where the first subscript determines a row and the second
subscript determines a column. For example "popmap[3,7]" refers to
the location in the 3rd row and the 7th column of the array. Thus
the declared array corresponds in size and shape to to the table
of data that we are considering.

To do something systematically with all the locations of a two-
dimensional array, we need to use a nested for-statement. For
example, if we wish to deal with the array a row at a time we need
the outline structure:

```
for row := 1 to 8 do

    deal with row
```

and dealing with a row involves a further loop:

```
for column := 1 to 10 do

    deal with the location popmap[row,column]
```

The next example illustrates this.

Program 8.10

This program reads the population table described above, stores it in a suitable array, calculates the total population and prints a copy of the population table.

```
program population(input,output);

var popmap : array [1..8,1..10] of integer;
    row, column, total : integer;

begin

    for row := 1 to 8 do
        for column := 1 to 10 do
            read(popmap[row,column]);


    total := 0;
    for row := 1 to 8 do
        for column := 1 to 10 do
            total := total + popmap[row,column];

    writeln('total population is ', total);   writeln;

    writeln('populations of individual zones are:');

    for row := 1 to 8 do
    begin
        writeln;
        for column := 1 to 10 do
            write(popmap[row,column]);
    end;

end.
```

The first nested for-statement causes the data to be read into the two-dimensional array "popmap", the second accesses the array, performing the required calculation, and the third causes the contents of the array to be printed. When the input for this program is being typed, the 10 numbers in the first row of the table are typed first and these are stored in the first row of the array. Then the 10 numbers in the second row are typed, and so on. Incidentally, the processes of reading the data and accumulating the total could have been carried out simultaneously, the first two boxes being merged into a single nested loop. This could not be easily done in the next program.

## Program 8.11

Reads data as in program 8.10. In addition it reads four numbers defining a sub-region on the map over which the population is to be added. For example, input of 2 6 3 5 specifies the region lying between rows 2 and 6 and between columns 3 and 5:

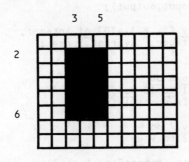

```
program popmap2(input,output);

var popmap : array [1..8,1..10] of integer;
    row, col, rowa, cola, rowb, colb, subtotal : integer;

begin
    for row := 1 to 8 do
        for col := 1 to 10 do
            read(popmap[row,col]);

    subtotal := 0;
    read(rowa, rowb, cola, colb);

    for row := rowa to rowb do
        for col := cola to colb do
            subtotal := subtotal + popmap[row,col];

    writeln('population of sub-zone is ', subtotal)
end.
```

## Program 8.12
Reads data as in Program 8.10 and finds every zone with a population less than half the average of its north, south, east and west neighbours.

```
program popmap3(input,output);

var popmap : array [1..8,1..10] of integer;
    row, col : integer;  average : real;

begin
    for row := 1 to 8 do
        for col := 1 to 10 do
        read(popmap[row,col]);

    for row := 2 to 7 do
        for col := 2 to 9 do
        begin
            average := (popmap[row-1,col]
                        +popmap[row+1,col]
                        +popmap[row,col-1]
                        +popmap[row,col+1])/4;
            if popmap[row,col] < average/2
            then writeln('the region ', row, col,
                        ' is underpopulated')
        end
end.
```

The next program illustrates random access to a two-dimensional array.

## Program 8.13
A student's week is divided up into 5 days, each of 6 periods numbered 1..6. He must attend 20 lectures during each week. The program reads a list of his lecture times and places. Each lecture time is represented by two integers giving the day (1..5) and the period (1..6) and these two integers are followed by the number of the room (a positive integer) in which the lecture takes place.

The program prints a timetable for the student in the form:

```
                  period

          1   2   3   4   5   6
         ----------------------
mon       3   1   2   9
tue       6   6   5   7   6
wed           2   1
thu       5   2   5       8   7
fri       3   2   1   3
```

where the entry for each period represents the room number in which he should be. We assume that the input data is such that there are no timetable clashes.

134

```
program times(input,output);

var day, period, room, lecture : integer;
    place : array [1..5,1..6] of integer;

begin

(* use zeros to mark all periods as free *)
    for day := 1 to 5 do
        for period := 1 to 6 do
            place[day,period] := 0;

(* now fill in appropriate periods with room number *)
    for lecture := 1 to 20 do
    begin
        read(day,period,room);
        place[day,period] := room;
    end;

(* now print the timetable *)
    writeln('period':28);
    writeln('1  2  3  4  5  6':34);
    writeln('----------------':34);

    for day := 1 to 5 do
    begin
        case day of
            1 : write('mon');
            2 : write('tue');
            3 : write('wed');
            4 : write('thu');
            5 : write('fri')
        end;

        write('              ');
        for period := 1 to 6 do
            if place[day,period] = 0 then
                        write('   ')
            else  write(place[day,period]:3);

        writeln
    end
end.
```

## 8.6 More about subscripts

Previously we have utilized arrays with the subscript range
starting at 1. There are many contexts in which we may require a
subscript range to start at some integer other than 1. Consider
again our price list example:

```
var priceof : array [1..100] of real;
```

Such a declaration would mean that we could use in our program the integers 1..100 as reference numbers. However the following declaration:

```
var priceof : array [99..199] of real;
```

would mean that we could use the integers 99..199 as reference numbers.

Program 8.14

A mail order company stocks 563 different items with reference numbers 3001 to 3563. The program reads a list of prices in order of reference number. The program then reads a list of items required by a customer. Each item is specified by a reference number followed by the quantity required, and the last item is followed immediately by the terminating character '*'. The total cost of the customer's order is printed.

```
program sale(input,output);

const minref = 3001; maxref = 3563;
var priceof : array [minref..maxref] of real;
    ref, nextref, quantity : integer;
    totalprice : real; nextch : char;

begin
    for nextref := minref to maxref do
        read(priceof[nextref]);

    totalprice := 0;
    repeat
        read(ref,quantity);
        totalprice := totalprice + priceof[ref]*quantity;
        read(nextch)
    until nextch = '*';

    writeln('total cost of order is ', totalprice)
end.
```

Note that in this example we have used two named constants to define the subscript range. A subscript range must be defined in terms of **constant** values, named or otherwise.

Finally we introduce in Program 8.15 the idea of using a character as a subscript.

136

Program 8.15
This program plots a histogram showing the frequency of occurrence
of each alphabetic character in a segment of text terminated by
'*'. We assume that no scaling is necessary in the histogram.

```
program freqcount(input,output);

var lettercount : array ['a'..'z'] of integer;
    letter, character : char; col : integer;

begin
    for letter := 'a' to 'z' do
        lettercount[letter] := 0;

    read(character);
    repeat
        if character in ['a'..'z'] then
            lettercount[character]:=lettercount[character]+1;
        read(character);
    until character = '*';

    for letter := 'a' to 'z' do
    begin
        writeln;
        for col := 1 to lettercount[letter] do
        write('*')
    end
end.
```

Exercises for Chapter 8

1) Write a program similar to Program 8.2 but which reads a price
list for 100 items from a file. The program is then to read a
list of quantities required by a customer, for example:

| | | |
|---|---|---|
| 5 | means | 5 of item 1 |
| 10 | means | 10 of item 2 |
| 0 | means | 0 of item 3 |
| 12 | means | 12 of item 4 |
| . | . | |
| . | . | |
| 27 | means | 27 of item 100 |

The program should calculate the total cost of the customer's
order.

2) As Exercise 1 but this time the customer's order is specified
as a list of pairs where each pair contains an item number
followed by the quantity required. The last quantity is
followed immediately by the character '*'. The item numbers
appear in any order. The program should check that each item
number input does in fact exist.

137

3) Write a program that reads a piece of text terminated by a '*' and finds the most frequently occuring letter in the text.

4) Write a program that will read an integer "n" followed by an n-letter word and which will determine whether or not the word is a palindrome. (A palindrome is a word that reads the same forwards and backwards e.g. ROTOR.)

5) Write a program which accepts input from a file of thirty daily temperature readings in the range -20 to 40. The program is to draw a graph of the following form:

```
1                        +    *
2                        + *
3                       *+
4              *    +
5                       *+
6                        +   *
7                        +      *
        etc.
```

where the distance of a '*' from the left represents a temperature reading and the position of the '+'s represents the average reading over the whole period.

6) Each day in a college's weekly timetable is divided into seven periods. The timetable for a course consists of a list of five periods during which the course is given, where a period is represented by two numbers, the first giving the day of the week (1 = Monday, 2 = Tuesday, etc.) and the second giving the number of the period on that day.

Write a program that accepts as input the timetables for the 6 courses a pupil wishes to attend, and which tells him whether he has any timetable clashes.

7) In a warehouse system, car parts are stored in a two-dimensional stack of pigeonholes, fifty columns long and ten rows high. This unit is accessed by an automatic electromechanical fetch unit which is given a pair of coordinates by a computer when a part is to be fetched. The values of the elements of a two dimensional array are to represent the number of items in the pigeonholes and this array should be initialized from a file.

Write a program which repeatedly:

a) accepts a reference number in the range 1..500 and outputs the corresponding pair of coordinates (successive reference numbers are to correspond to consecutive pigeon holes in a row-wise manner starting at the top left pigeonhole);

b) decrements the appropriate array location by one, thus keeping an up to date stock record;

c) writes an appropriate message if the stock in a pigeonhole falls below ten items.

138

The input reference numbers will be terminated by a '*'
immediately after the last number. At this point the program
should print a two-dimensional representation of the stack,
printing a '-' for the pigeonholes in which the stock has
fallen below ten items and printing a '+' for the others.

8) A particular photo-micrograph contains a single simple convex
shape, such as a circle, represented as a dark area on a light
background. Such images are commonly represented in computers
as two-dimensional arrays, where each element has the value 1
or 0. A dark area on a light background becomes a group of 1's
surrounded by 0's.

   Write a program that will accept such an array as input. The
program should display the shape of the dark region by
printing the points on the boundary as 1's and the background
and interior points as spaces. Test your program on a 10x10
array.
   Hint: Scan the image row-wise or column-wise. For a given 1,
if any of the surrounding points are 0's, then that 1
represents a boundary point.

9) Write a program that accepts as input a photomicrograph of the
type described in Exercise 8. The program should calculate the
ratio of the area of the dark region to its perimeter. As a
measure of the area, count the number of ones. A (rather
inaccurate) measure of the perimeter can be obtained by
counting the number of boundary points and you should use this
in your program. As a more difficult exercise, you might like
to think about how to obtain a more accurate measure of the
length of the boundary. (Two diagonally adjacent boundary
points would make a contribution of sqrt(2) to such a
measure.)

# 9 Giving a process a name: simple procedures

A procedure is a section of program to which a name has been given. The programmer can then write the name of the procedure wherever he wants that section of program to be obeyed. This has two main advantages:

Firstly, if the named operation has to be carried out at several different places in a large program, we avoid writing out the same section of program in full at each place.

Secondly, careful use of procedures can make a large program easier to write and easier for other people to read. For example, in a payroll program we might have a sequence of operations such as

```
addnormalhourspay;
addovertimehourspay;
deductincometax
```

where the details of each named operation are defined elsewhere. This makes it much easier to understand what the program is doing than would be the case if the program text for each calculation were written out in full here.

## 9.1 Introductory example

We shall introduce the idea of giving a name to a section of PASCAL program by means of a very simple example. We shall write a program which reads two numbers and indicates whether or not the first is larger than the second. As in Program 7.10, the input may include extraneous text before and between the numbers. This extra text is to be ignored. Thus, for example, given input:

is the number 36 bigger than 432?

the output might be:

first number is not bigger.

We present a description of what the program must do as follows:

```
writeln('type in your enquiry.');

findstartofnumber;

read(firstnumber);

findstartofnumber;

read(secondnumber);
if firstnumber > secondnumber then
    writeln('first number is bigger.')
else
    writeln('first number is not bigger.')
```

Here the process of finding the start of a number in the input  is
to be carried  out  at  two different points in the program. We
therefore refer to this process  by name  - "findstartofnumber" -
wherever  it  is required, and define this process elsewhere. This
process involves reading and ignoring characters until  the  next
unread  character  in  the  input is a numeric digit. As in Program
7.10, this can be written:

```
while not (input↑ in ['0'..'9']) do
    get(input)
```

Each occurrence of  "findstartofnumber" in the  outline  program
could be replaced by this statement. Instead, we shall give a name
to  this  process by writing it separately in a **procedure
declaration:**

```
procedure findstartofnumber;
begin
    while not (input↑ in ['0'..'9']) do
        get(input)
end;
```

This  procedure  declaration  is  inserted  after  the  variable
declarations  at  the start of the program. "findstartofnumber" is
the name of the procedure and we can insert an instruction  to  go
and  obey  the  procedure  at  any  point in the program by simply
writing the name of the procedure. Such an instruction is known as
a **procedure call.**

```
```

Program 9.1
The complete program looks like this.

```
program compare(input,output);

var firstnumber,secondnumber : integer;

    procedure findstartofnumber;
    begin
        while not (input↑ in ['0'..'9']) do
            get(input)
    end;

begin
    writeln('type in your enquiry.');

    findstartofnumber;

    read(firstnumber);

    findstartofnumber;

    read(secondnumber);
    if firstnumber > secondnumber then
        writeln('first number is bigger.')
    else
        writeln('first number is not bigger.')
end.
```

When the computer executes this program, the first statement obeyed is the first statement in the list between the main begin...end of the program. The instructions within the procedure declaration are not obeyed until a procedure call is encountered. Thus the above program behaves as if the text of the procedure definition were substituted in place of each call of the procedure. Obeying the above program is equivalent in effect to obeying:

```
writeln('type in your enquiry.');

while not (input↑ in ['0'..'9']) do
    get(input);

read(firstnumber);

while not (input↑ in ['0'..'9']) do
    get(input);

read(secondnumber);
if firstnumber > secondnumber then
    writeln('first number is bigger.')
else
    writeln('first number is not bigger.')
```

142

Notice that the structure of a procedure declaration is rather
like that of a miniature program. In fact a procedure can contain
declarations of constants and variables intended for use only
within itself. It can even contain a further procedure
declaration. The following program illustrates the declaration of
variables within a procedure.

Program 9.2
A manufacturer has two identical machines, each of which is
producing ball-bearings. The diameters of a sample of 10 ball
bearings from the first machine are to be typed as input to a
computer program and are to be followed by the diameters of a
sample of 10 ball-bearings from the second machine. This program
accepts the two sets of 10 measurements. It calculates and prints
the average of the first 10 values, the average of the second 10
values and then prints the overall average for the 20 values
supplied.

```
program average20(input,output);

var overallsum : real;

    procedure average10;
    var count : integer;  next, sum10 : real;
    begin
        sum10 := 0;
        for count := 1 to 10 do
        begin
            read(next);
            sum10 := sum10 + next
        end;
        writeln('average of 10 readings :', sum10/10);
        overallsum := overallsum + sum10
    end;

begin
    overallsum := 0;
    average10;
    average10;
    writeln('overall average :', overallsum/20)
end.
```

In the above program, the variable "overallsum" is declared at
the start of the program and can be used anywhere in the program,
even within the procedure. Such a variable is called a **global**
variable. The variables "count", "next", and "sum10" on the other
hand are used only within the procedure "average10" and are
therefore declared within this procedure. Variables declared at
the start of a procedure in this way can not be used outside the
procedure definition. We describe the variables "count", "next"
and "sum10" as being **local** to the procedure. Storage space for
these variables is allocated each time the procedure is called and
the space is freed for possible use by other variables elsewhere
in the program when the procedure terminates. It is recommended

that any variable which is used only within a particular procedure should be declared locally to that procedure. The computer will then ensure that the programmer does not accidentally use the same variable for conflicting purposes in different parts of a large program.

In the above programs, defining a procedure saved us from writing exactly the same piece of program out in detail twice. In Chapter 10, we shall explain how a procedure can be given "parameters" telling it which values or variables to process on a particular occasion. The same procedure can then be used to perform similar, but not necessarily identical, operations on different occasions. For the moment, we wish to draw attention to another application of simple procedures - their use in making programs easier to write and easier to read. In the remaining sections of this chapter, we use two character-processing examples to illustrate this idea.

## 9.2 A text analysis example

The student of language or literature often makes use of a computer to analyze a piece of text which he is studying. Writers all have unconscious habits of style - the frequency with which they use certain words, the average length of their sentences and so on - and these features can be easily detected by a computer program. Thus, in cases of disputed authorship, for example, a computer analysis can be used to demonstrate that two pieces of text were probably written by the same person.

As a simple example, let us write a program which calculates the average number of words per sentence in a piece of text. We shall assume that words in the text are separated by one or more non-alphabetic characters and that words contain only alphabetic characters. For convenience, we shall assume that a sentence is terminated by a full stop immediately after the last word in the sentence and that the text is terminated by the character '*' immediately after the last full stop. The program is to report separately the number of words in each sentence encountered, and finally report the average number of words per sentence.

As suggested in Chapter 6, we start by writing an outline description of the process that we want to program, giving meaningful names to any sub-processes involved. Programming these sub-processes can then be tackled in the same way, almost as if they were separate programming problems. By adopting this technique of stepwise refinement, we never get involved in considering a program or section of program in more detail than our minds can cope with at one time. In this case, we can outline what the program should do as follows:

```
noofsentences := 0;
totalwords := 0;

repeat
    processasentence;
    noofsentences := noofsentences + 1
until input↑ = '*';

writeln('average number of words per sentence = ',
        totalwords/noofsentences)
```

At this stage in planning the program, we have clear in our minds
an outline picture of the structure of the program - a loop, each
execution of which processes a sentence. We can now concentrate on
describing in further detail the operation referred to as
"processasentence":

```
sentencewords := 0;

repeat
    findstartofword;
    readword;
    sentencewords := sentencewords + 1
until input↑ = '.';

get(input); (* remove the full stop from the input *)
writeln('next sentence: ', sentencewords, ' words');
totalwords := totalwords + sentencewords
```

We can now see that processing a sentence involves repeatedly
finding the start of the next word and then reading the word
itself, a word being counted after it has been read. Only when
this is clear should we proceed to the next stage and consider in
detail the processes "findstartofword" and "readword":

To find the start of a word, we require

```
while not (input↑ in ['a'..'z']) do
    get(input)
```

We use a while-statement in case there are no spaces before the
first word. To read a word we require

```
repeat
    get(input)
until not (input↑ in ['a'..'z'])
```

The complete program could now be written without using procedures by replacing the line

```
processasentence;
```

by the more detailed description of this process, in which the lines

```
findstartofword;
```

and

```
readword;
```

are replaced by the appropriate statements. However, we prefer to make the structure of the program match the way in which it was designed. Each process to which a name was given while planning the program is defined as a separate procedure. This makes the program considerably easier to understand or modify at a later date, because the different stages involved in planning the program correspond clearly to separate sections of the text of the program. This is particularly important if, as is often the case, the person responsible for maintaining and modifying a program is not the original programmer.

Program 9.3
A complete program to calculate the average length of sentence in
a piece of text.

```pascal
program sentenceanalysis(input,output);

var totalwords, noofsentences :integer;

    procedure processasentence;

    var sentencewords : integer;

        procedure findstartofword;
        begin
            while not (input↑ in ['a'..'z']) do
                get(input)
        end;

        procedure readword;
        begin
            repeat
                get(input)
            until not (input↑ in ['a'..'z'])
        end;

    begin
        sentencewords := 0;

        repeat
            findstartofword;
            readword;
            sentencewords := sentencewords + 1
        until input↑ = '.';

        get(input); (* remove full stop from input *)
        writeln('next sentence: ',
                        sentencewords, ' words');
        totalwords := totalwords + sentencewords
    end;

begin (* main block of program *)
    noofsentences := 0;
    totalwords := 0;

    repeat
        processasentence;
        noofsentences := noofsentences + 1
    until input↑ = '*';

    writeln('average number of words per sentence = ',
            totalwords/noofsentences)
end.
```

When attempting to read and understand a program like the above, always start by looking at the main **block** of the program between the main begin...end. Once the outline structure of the program is clear, you can then go on to examine any procedures which are called from the main block. These procedures should be approached in the same way - first read the main block of the procedure definition and only then go on to look at the definitions of the procedures which are called there. By doing this you will be working through the program in the same order as that in which it was originally written.

## 9.3 A word processing example

Word processors are now widely used in business for the preparation of letters and documents. Documents are initially typed into a disk or tape file. Subsequently a high quality output terminal can be used to produce as many copies of the document as are required. A further advantage of storing a document in this way is that programs can be used to edit the document or to change its layout. For example, in a stored document we may wish to replace every occurrence of the word "consulate" by the word "embassy". This book was typed into a word processor which was then used to improve the layout of the text in preparation for photographic reproduction. On a commercial word processor some of these editing and formatting programs may be activated simply by pressing an appropriate key.

The following program illustrates how we can change the layout of a piece of text on a word-by-word basis.

Let us assume that a piece of text has been typed into a file. We require a program to print it with the same line by line layout but with the punctuation printed in a "standard form". In the stored file, between two words there may be

a) one or more spaces

or b) a punctuation mark (comma, semicolon or full stop) surrounded by any number (zero or more) spaces.

The end of a line may appear anywhere between two words. The file is to be printed in such a way that two words are separated by

a) one space or the end of a line

or b) a punctuation mark followed by one space or the end of a line.

An outline of what the program should do is

```
processpunctuation;
repeat
   copyaword;
   processpunctuation
until eof(input)
```

where "processpunctuation" involves reading and dealing with
characters until either an alphabetic character is encountered or
until the end of the input file has been reached. This poses a
slight difficulty. Evaluation of a test such as

(input↑ in ['a'..'z']) or eof(input)

would fail when the end-of-file has been reached: the computer
will still attempt to look at the value "input↑" which is of
course undefined at that point. In order to avoid this difficulty,
the above condition has to be evaluated in two stages by using an
if-statement, the result of the test being stored in a boolean
variable:

```
endofpunctuation := false;
repeat
   if eof(input) then endofpunctuation := true
   else
      if input↑ in ['a'..'z'] then
         endofpunctuation := true
      else
              .
              .
              .

until endofpunctuation
```

"processpunctuation" must also watch out for an end-of-line.
Another boolean variable can be used to record when this happens
and, after all the punctuation has been read, the value of this
variable indicates whether a space or end-of-line should be
inserted in the output before the next word.

The procedure "copyaword" is straightforward and the complete
program becomes:

Program 9.4

```pascal
program textidy(input,output);

   procedure processpunctuation;

   var newlinemet, endofpunctuation : boolean;
      nextchar : char;

   begin
      newlinemet := false;
      endofpunctuation := false;
      repeat
         if eof(input) then endofpunctuation := true
         else
            if input↑ in ['a'..'z'] then
               endofpunctuation := true
            else
               if eoln(input) then
               begin
                  newlinemet := true; get(input)
               end
               else
               begin
                  read(nextchar);
                  if nextchar in [',', ';', '.'] then
                     write(nextchar)
               end
      until endofpunctuation;

      if newlinemet then writeln
      else write(' ')
   end;


   procedure copyaword;

   var nextchar : char;

   begin
      repeat
         read(nextchar);  write(nextchar)
      until not (input↑ in ['a'..'z'])
   end;

begin  (* main block of program *)
   processpunctuation;
   repeat
      copyaword;
      processpunctuation
   until eof(input)
end.
```

1) Write a program that reads three numbers, embedded in extraneous text, and which prints the largest and smallest of the three numbers. For example, if we assume that the numbers represent ages, input of

   john is 3 years old.
   mary's age is 7,
   william is 9.

   could result in output of

   the oldest is 9 years old.
   the youngest is 3 years old.

   Your program should incorporate the procedure used in Program 9.1.

2) A company's employees are paid £2.73 per hour for a standard 35-hour week. Overtime hours during the week are paid at 1.25 times this rate and overtime hours at the weekend are paid at 1.5 times this rate. Income tax is paid at a rate of 30% on the first £20 of a week's pay, 40% on the next £30 and 50% on the remainder. Write a program which accepts, as input, the number of weekday overtime hours worked and the number of weekend overtime hours worked by an employee in one week. The program should print a payslip giving details of his normal pay, overtime pay and deductions for that week. The main part of your program should consist of the three procedure-calls presented in the introduction to this chapter.

3) Modify Program 9.3 so that it reports the number of words in the shortest sentence found in the text, and the number of words in the longest sentence found in the text.

4) A bank normally levies charges on a customer's account at the rate of 20p per debit entry. However, charges are waived if the daily balance never falls below £50 over a 30-day period. A day's transactions on an account are recorded as a list of positive and negative numbers representing credit and debit entries on the account. Each numerical entry is on a separate line and is preceded on the line by a group of twenty characters describing the transaction. Such a daily list is terminated by the character '*' immediately after the last numerical entry. 30 such lists covering a period of 30 consecutive days have been typed one after another into a file and the amount of the customer's previous balance has been typed at the start of the file. Write a program that prints the customer's bank statement for the 30-day period. Use procedures to make the logical structure of your program clear.

5) A piece of text has been typed into a file with little attention being paid to the spacing between words or to the line-by-line layout of the text. (For the purposes of this example, a "word" is any group of non-space characters.) The

last word in the text is terminated by the character '*'. Write a program which reads the text and prints it with an improved layout as follows:
  a) There should be no spaces at the start of a line and there should never be more than one space between words on a line.
  b) A new line should be started immediately after printing a word if more than 50 characters have already been printed on the current line.

The main part of your program should be:

```
repeat
    processspaces;
    copyaword
until input↑ = '*'
```

6) A legal document contains a number of sentences and it has been typed into a file with little attention being paid to its layout. The last word in each sentence is terminated by a full stop and the last full stop is followed immediately by the character '*'. The document is to be printed with the sentences numbered 1,2,3..., each sentence starting on a new line. The output document should otherwise satisfy the layout requirements specified in the previous exercise. Write a program to do this.

# 10 More about procedures and functions

In chapter 9, we saw how a section of program can be given a name by declaring it as a procedure. Each time such a simple procedure is called, the same piece of program is obeyed. In the present chapter we explain how a procedure can be supplied with a parameter or parameters indicating the values or variables on which it should operate on a particular occasion. This enables the same procedure to be used for carrying out similar, but not necessarily identical, operations on different occasions.

## 10.1 Simple parameters

Let us write a program that accepts as input two 4-digit electricity meter readings and prints a simple electricity bill. In outline we require:

```
read(previous, present);
writeln('prev reading    pres reading     total due');
write previous meter reading;
write present  meter reading;
write total ammount due
```

Clearly the last three lines could all be replaced by simple write statements. However, it is usual on an electricity bill to display all the digits of a meter reading even if there are zeros at the start. For example, a reading of 56 should be printed as 0056. We shall therefore define our own procedure "write4digits" for printing a meter reading with all 4 digits displayed. When called, this procedure will be given a **parameter** telling it which value to print:

```
read(previous, present);
writeln('prev reading    pres reading      total due');
write4digits(previous);   write('   ');
write4digits(present);
writeln('£':8, (present - previous)*unitprice :5:2)
```

Here we require the procedure "write4digits" to be obeyed on one occasion using the value of "previous" and on a second occasion using the value of "present". This procedure can be written:

```
procedure write4digits(meterreading : integer);
begin
    write('      ');
    if meterreading < 10 then write('000')
    else if meterreading < 100 then write('00')
    else if meterreading < 1000 then write('0');
    write(meterreading)
end;
```

In this procedure definition, or **declaration,** the operation to be
carried out by the procedure is specified in terms of
"meterreading", which is a parameter. When the procedure is
called, this parameter is given an actual value which is to be
used when the procedure is obeyed. Thus, obeying the statement

```
write4digits(previous)
```

causes the procedure definition to be obeyed with the parameter
"meterreading" set to the value of the variable "previous".
Similarly,

```
write4digits(present)
```

causes the procedure to be obeyed with the parameter
"meterreading" set to the value of the variable "present".
Incidentally, the same procedure could also be called by

```
write4digits(256 + 17)
```

which would result in output of 0273.

A parameter supplied in brackets when the procedure is called
is usually referred to as an **actual parameter.**

The complete electricity bill program is:

154

Program <u>10.1</u>

```
    program electricitybill(input,output);

    const unitprice = 0.034;

    var previous, present : integer;

        procedure write4digits(meterreading : integer);
        begin
            write('        ');
            if meterreading < 10 then write('000')
            else if meterreading < 100 then write('00')
            else if meterreading < 1000 then write('0');
            write(meterreading)
        end;

    begin
        read(previous, present);
        writeln('prev reading   pres reading    total due');
        write4digits(previous);  write('    ');
        write4digits(present);
        writeln('£':8, (present - previous)*unitprice :5:2)
    end.
```

As an example of a procedure with two parameters, consider:

```
    procedure writechar(ch : char;  nooftimes : integer);
    var count : integer;
    begin
        for count:= 1 to nooftimes do write(ch);
        writeln
    end;
```

This procedure is defined in terms of two parameters, "ch" and "nooftimes". In this case, these are of different types, and parameters of different types must be separated from each other in the procedure heading by semicolons.

When this procedure is called, the character supplied as its first parameter is printed a number of times which is specified as a value for the second parameter. For example, if we call the procedure as follows:

```
    writechar('*', 5)
```

"ch" is given the value '*' and "nooftimes" is given the value 5 and the procedure definition is obeyed. Output is therefore:

*****

Notice that when a procedure is called, the actual parameters used in the procedure call are always separated by commas.

The actual parameters supplied to this procedure can in fact be any two expressions, provided that the first represents a character and the second represents an integer. For example, if "symbol" is a character variable and "noofsymbols" is an integer variable, then the fragment:

```
symbol := 'a';  noofsymbols := 5;
writechar(symbol, noofsymbols);
writechar(succ(succ(symbol)), 2*noofsymbols + 1)
```

will output

aaaaa
ccccccccccc

If "letter" is an "array[1..4] of char" and "noofletter" is an "array[1..4] of integer", then the fragment:

```
letter[1] := 'w';  letter[2] := 'x';
letter[3] := 'y';  letter[4] := 'z';

noofletter[1] :=  5;  noofletter[2] := 10;
noofletter[3] := 15;  noofletter[4] := 20;

for i := 1 to 4 do
    writechar(letter[i], noofletter[i])
```

will output

wwwww
xxxxxxxxxx
yyyyyyyyyyyyyyy
zzzzzzzzzzzzzzzzzzzz

As we have seen, the type of each parameter of a procedure must be specified in the procedure heading. However, when a procedure involves a group of parameters of the same type, the names of these parameters can be listed together, separated by commas, with the type specified once at the end of the list. Parameters of different types still have to be separated from each other by semicolons. The following example of a procedure heading should make this clear:

```
procedure demo(i,j :integer;  a,b,c,d :char;  x,y,z :real);

begin

        definition of the procedure

end;
```

Remember that all parameters are separated by commas when the procedure is called. This procedure could be called as follows:

```
demo(256, 73, '*', 'p', 'q', 'r', 26.45, 72.6, 18.253)
```

As was the case with the simple procedures of Chapter 9, a procedure definition can include declarations of variables, or even other procedures, for its own local use.


Program 10.2

This program reads two positive integers and prints them in descending order. The integers are to be output on separate lines and, when an integer is output, the millions are to be followed by a comma and the thousands are to be followed by a comma. Thus, instead of writing 5674251 the program should write 5,671,251 (This program will not work on a PASCAL system where the maximum permitted integer is less than 1000000.)

```
program compare(input,output);

var first, second : integer;

    procedure commawrite(n : integer);
    var millions, thousands, units : integer;

        procedure zerowrite(m : integer);
        begin
            if m < 100 then write('0');
            if m < 10 then write('0');
            write(m)
        end;

    begin
        millions := n div 1000000;
        thousands := (n mod 1000000) div 1000;
        units := n mod 1000;
        if millions > 0 then
        begin
            write(millions, ',');
            zerowrite(thousands); write(',');
            zerowrite(units)
        end
        else
            if thousands > 0 then
            begin
                write(thousands, ',');
                zerowrite(units)
            end
            else write(units);

        writeln
    end;

begin
    read(first, second);
    if first > second then
    begin
        commawrite(first);  commawrite(second)
    end
    else
    begin
        commawrite(second);  commawrite(first)
    end
end.
```

In attempting to write a program like the above, or in attempting to understand a program that someone else has written, always remember to start with the main body of the program (between the main begin...end). Once this has been dealt with, any procedures called in the main body of the program can be treated in the same way, then any procedures called by these procedures, and so on. In this case, the main body of the program is straightforward, provided that we avoid getting bogged down in the problems involved in printing a number with the commas inserted.

Designing the procedure "commawrite" can then be viewed as a programming problem which is rather easier than the original problem. The need for the procedure "zerowrite" arises because, for example, a number of thousands has to be written with a full three digits in the context of a number like 2,067,003. In the number 67,003 the thousands are printed with no extra zeros, and a normal write-statement is used.

Now read through the above program in this way and ensure that you understand it.

## 10.2 A programming-language translation example

In this section, we illustrate further the use of simple parameters, using as an example the idea of translating from one programming-language to another. The electronic circuits in a computer are designed to respond to instructions expressed in a very primitive programming language known as the machine-code of the computer. In order that the computer can be given instructions in a high-level language such as PASCAL, someone has to write a computer program which can analyze a PASCAL program and arrange for the computer to carry out the operations that have been specified in PASCAL. One way of doing this is to write a program which can translate a PASCAL program into equivalent machine-code instructions, which the computer subsequently obeys.

Here we provide a very simple introduction to the idea of programming-language translation by writing a program which will read an expression such as

a+x*z

and will print instructions for evaluating the expression on a simple pocket calculator, for example:

key in the value for x
press the multiplication key
key in the value for z
press the addition key
key in the value for a
display the answer

We shall assume, for simplicity, that an input expression contains exactly two operators and three variable names and that brackets are not permitted. Each variable name is a single letter and the expression is typed without any additional spaces between the symbols.

The program has to decide which operator to apply first. In the above example, '*' has greater priority than '+', and, when evaluating the expression, the multiplication must be done first. If the first operator has the greater priority or if both operators have the same priority, the first operator is applied first. In outline, we require:

```
if (op2 in ['*', '/']) and (op1 in ['+', '-']) then
    output instructions for applying the second
        operator before the first
else
    output instructions for applying the first
        operator before the second
```

We can describe this process in a little more detail as follows:

```
if (op2 in ['*', '/']) and (op1 in ['+', '-']) then
begin
    valueof(var2);
    apply(op2);
    valueof(var3);
    apply(op1);
    valueof(var1)
end
else
begin
    valueof(var1);
    apply(op1);
    valueof(var2);
    apply(op2);
    valueof(var3)
end
```

Here, "valueof" is going to be a procedure which outputs an
instruction to key in the value of a variable, the name of the
variable (a letter) being supplied as a parameter. "apply" is a
procedure which outputs an instruction to press an appropriate
operation key, the operation symbol ('+', '-', '*' or '/') being
supplied as a parameter. Defining these procedures, we get the
complete program:

## Program 10.3

```
program evaluate(input, output);

var var1, op1, var2, op2, var3 : char;

    procedure valueof(variable : char);

    begin
        writeln('key in the value for ', variable)
    end;


    procedure apply(op : char);

    begin
        write('press the ');
        case op of
            '+': write('addition');
            '-': write('subtraction');
            '*': write('multiplication');
            '/': write('division')
        end;
        writeln(' key')
    end;

begin
    read(var1, op1, var2, op2, var3);

    if (op2 in ['*', '/']) and (op1 in ['+', '-']) then
    begin
        valueof(var2);
        apply(op2);
        valueof(var3);
        apply(op1);
        valueof(var1)
    end
    else
    begin
        valueof(var1);
        apply(op1);
        valueof(var2);
        apply(op2);
        valueof(var3)
    end;

    writeln('display the answer.')
end.
```

## 10.3 Variable parameters

In the procedures of the previous two sections, a parameter was always used for specifying a **value** which was to be processed when the procedure is called. As another example of this, consider the following procedure declaration:

```
procedure process(x : integer);
begin
    writeln(x);
    writeln(x*x)
end;
```

When this procedure is called, the parameter corresponding to "x" can be any expression representing an integer **value**. For example, provided that the variable "a" and the array location "mark[2,3]" each contain an integer value, then each of the following statements are valid calls of this procedure:

```
process(5742);
process(a);
process(a*5 + 32);
process(mark[2,3]);
process(mark[2,3]*3 + 564)
```

When a procedure is called, a simple parameter can be used only for transferring information **into** the procedure. We sometimes require to use a parameter to transfer information **out** of the procedure back to the calling section of program. This is done by giving the procedure a **variable** parameter which tells the procedure where to put the required information. Let us return to the vote counting example used in Chapter 5 - Program 5.9. We will extend this program to print a message indicating who has won the election. An outline of what the program must do is as follows:

```
add up the votes for one
    party and put the total in "party1overall" ;
add up the votes for the other
    party and put the total in "party2overall" ;

if party1overall = party2overall then
    writeln('a draw.')
else if party1overall > party2overall then
        writeln('a win for party 1.')
        else writeln('a win for party 2.')
```

Clearly, the two processes involved in the first section of the above outline are similar. In the first case, we want to read and add numbers, placing the total in the variable "party1overall", and in the second case, we want to perform exactly the same operation except that the total is to be placed in "party2overall". We shall define a procedure "addupvotesfor" which can be used as follows:

```
addupvotesfor(party1overall);
addupvotesfor(party2overall)
```

Here, we require the procedure to place a value in a **variable**, which is supplied as a parameter when the procedure is called, and this has to be indicated in the procedure heading.

Program 10.4
This is Program 5.9 rewritten to use a procedure.

```
program election3(input,output);

var party1overall, party2overall : integer;

    procedure addupvotesfor(var total : integer);

    var next : integer;

    begin
        total := 0;
        read(next);
        repeat
            total := total + next;
            read(next)
        until next < 0
    end;

begin
    addupvotesfor(party1overall);
    addupvotesfor(party2overall);

    if party1overall = party2overall then
        writeln('a draw.')
    else if party1overall > party2overall then
            writeln('a win for party 1.')
            else writeln('a win for party 2.')
end.
```

In general, if a procedure is to be called with the intention of changing one of its parameters by assigning a value to that parameter or by reading a value into it, then that parameter must be preceded by the word <u>var</u> in the procedure heading. This is the case with the parameter "total" in the above program. When the procedure is called by

```
addupvotesfor(party1overall)
```

the procedure is obeyed with "total" referring to the same storage
location as "party1overall". Thus, whenever the statement

```
total := total + next
```

is obeyed, the computer behaves on this occasion as if it was
obeying

```
party1overall := party1overall + next
```

The result of obeying the procedure on this occasion is to add up
the first set of votes supplied as input, the total being
accumulated in "party1overall". Later, when the procedure is
obeyed as a result of

```
addupvotesfor(party2overall)
```

each reference to "total" behaves like a reference to
"party2overall". This call of the procedure thus adds up the
second set of votes in the input, accumulating the total in
"party2overall".

It would clearly be **wrong** for a call of the procedure
"addupvotesfor" to have a constant or expression as its parameter:

```
addupvotesfor(3);
addupvotesfor(party1overall + party2overall)
```

The procedure expects to be told **where to put** a value and must
therefore be given the name of a variable or an array location as
its actual parameter. We could declare an array such as

```
var party : array [1..3] of integer;
```

and call the procedure by, for example,

```
addupvotesfor(party[1]);
addupvotesfor(party[2]);
addupvotesfor(party[3])
```

or equivalently

164

```
for next := 1 to 3 do
    addupvotesfor(party[next])
```

In this case, three sets of votes would have to be supplied as input.

There is no reason why a procedure should not be supplied with an actual var parameter which already has a value stored in it. Any such value may be operated on during the execution of the procedure. As an example, we will write a program which reads three numbers and prints them in descending order. To do this, the numbers will be read and stored in the order in which they are input in three variables: "first", "second" and "third". The program will then rearrange the numbers as follows:

```
order the two numbers in "first" and "second";
(* this may involve swapping their contents *)

order the two numbers now in "first" and "third";
(* "first" now contains the largest number *)

order the two numbers now in "second" and "third"
```

We shall define a procedure which will examine the contents of two specified variables and, if necessary, swap their contents so as to ensure that the larger number is in the first variable and the smaller number is in the other. This procedure will be used as follows:

```
order(first, second);
order(first, third);
order(second, third)
```

The complete program therefore becomes:

Program 10.5

```pascal
program sort3numbers(input,output);

var first, second, third : integer;

    procedure order(var a,b : integer);

    var temp : integer;

    begin
        if a < b then
        begin
            temp := a;
            a := b;
            b := temp
        end
    end;

begin
    read(first, second, third);
    order(first, second);
    order(first, third);
    order(second, third);
    writeln(first:6, second:6, third:6)
end.
```

Finally, note that in a procedure heading variable parameters must be grouped separately from other parameters, the groups being separated from each other by semicolons. The following procedure takes two values and puts their sum in one variable and their product in another:

```pascal
procedure addandmultiply(value1, value2 : real;
                         var sum, product : real);
begin
    sum := value1 + value2;
    product := value1 * value2
end;
```

This procedure might be called as follows:

```pascal
var x, y, sum1, prod1 : real;
    a, b : array [1..10] of real;
    .
    .

    addandmultiply(3.4, 7.2, x, y);
    addandmultiply(x + 3.7, y + 4.3, sum1, prod1);
    addandmultiply(23.72, 63.15, a[1], b[1])
    .
    .
```

166

## 10.4 Array parameters

In this section, we describe how an array can be used as the parameter of a procedure. To introduce the techniques required, consider the following simple problem.

Fred and Joe have each taken six examination papers. Write a program which will read the six marks obtained by Fred followed by the six marks obtained by Joe. The program should calculate the total marks obtained by each candidate and should then print the six individual paper marks and the total mark for each candidate. The marks for the candidate with the higher total mark should be printed first.

The outline structure of this program will be as follows:

```
var fredsmarks, joesmarks : array [1..6] of integer;
    fredstotal, joestotal : integer;
    .
    .
begin
    readandadd(fredsmarks, fredstotal);
    readandadd(joesmarks, joestotal);
    if fredstotal > joestotal then
    begin
        write('fred: '); writeout(fredsmarks, fredstotal);
        write('joe: '); writeout(joesmarks,  joestotal )
    end
    else
    begin
        write('joe: '); writeout(joesmarks,  joestotal );
        write('fred: '); writeout(fredsmarks, fredstotal)
    end
end.
```

The procedure call

```
readandadd(fredsmarks, fredstotal)
```

is intended to read 6 numbers into the array "fredsmarks" and add these numbers together, putting the total in "fredstotal". This procedure will be defined in terms of two parameters - an array of six locations and an integer variable - and in the procedure declaration, these parameters must be specified as such. However, a complex type description such as "array[1..6] of integer" must not be used to specify the type of a procedure parameter. Only named types can be used in procedure headings and the above type must be given a name by inserting a line such as

```
type marklist = array [1..6] of integer;
```

at the start of the program. The name "marklist" can then be used
throughout the rest of the program to describe such an array of
six integers and the procedure definition becomes:

```
procedure readandadd(var markfor : marklist;
                     var total : integer);

var nextpaper : integer;
begin
    total := 0;
    for nextpaper := 1 to 6 do
    begin
        read(markfor[nextpaper]);
        total := total + markfor[nextpaper]
    end
end;
```

The declaration in the outline program can also be more
concisely expressed:

```
var fredsmarks, joesmarks : marklist;
    fredstotal, joestotal : integer;
```

For various reasons, an array parameter should always be
specified as a var parameter, except in rare circumstances, a
discussion of which is beyond the scope of this book. The effect
of this is that a procedure is always told **where to find** an array
rather than being given all the values stored in it.

We now present the complete program:

Program <u>10.6</u>

```
program exam(input, output);

type marklist = array[1..6] of integer;

var fredsmarks, joesmarks : marklist;
    fredstotal, joestotal : integer;

    procedure readandadd(var markfor : marklist;
                         var total : integer);

    var nextpaper : integer;

    begin
       total := 0;
       for nextpaper := 1 to 6 do
       begin
          read(markfor[nextpaper]);
          total := total + markfor[nextpaper]
       end
    end;

    procedure writeout(var markfor : marklist;
                       total : integer);

    var nextpaper : integer;

    begin
       for nextpaper := 1 to 6 do
          write(markfor[nextpaper] : 3);
       writeln('   total: ', total)
    end;

begin
   readandadd(fredsmarks, fredstotal);
   readandadd(joesmarks, joestotal);
   if fredstotal > joestotal then
   begin
      write('fred: '); writeout(fredsmarks, fredstotal);
      write('joe: '); writeout(joesmarks, joestotal )
   end
   else
   begin
      write('joe: '); writeout(joesmarks, joestotal );
      write('fred: '); writeout(fredsmarks, fredstotal)
   end
end.
```

Finally, note that the declarations at the head of a program or at the head of a procedure or function (see next section) must be in the following order:

1) const declarations
2) type declarations
3) var declarations
4) procedure and function declarations.

## 10.5 Functions

If the result of some process is a single value then a function is sometimes an elegant alternative to a procedure. We have already seen how to use the standard functions "sqrt", "sqr", "sin", "cos" and so on.

First let us look at the ways in which a function differs from a procedure. Certainly, they are both separate modules of program text referred to by name, but they differ in the way in which they are called. Functions are called by using them in arithmetic expressions – that is the first difference. The second difference is that the result of obeying the function is a single value which replaces the function call in the originating expression. Let us illustrate this by considering:

```
y := x + sqrt(2)
```

When this statement is being obeyed, the computer obeys the definition of the function "sqrt", and a number – the result of obeying the function – replaces the subexpression "sqrt(2)". In the case of a standard function like "sqrt", the definition of the function is already stored as part of the PASCAL system, but it is also possible for the programmer to define his own functions. They are declared at the start of a program in a way similar to that in which procedures are declared. A function declared in this way can then be used in exactly the same way as the standard functions.

## Program 10.7
This program reads 3 pairs of numbers and adds the larger of the first pair, the larger of the second pair and the larger of the third pair.

```
program add(input,output);

var a,b,p,q,x,y : real;

    function max(first,second : real) : real;

    begin
        if first > second then max := first
        else max := second
    end (* of max *);

begin
    read(a,b, p,q, x,y);
    writeln(max(a,b) + max(p,q) + max(x,y))
end.
```

The effect of calling a function is the calculation of a single
result. The result has a type which must be specified. This is
done by writing the name of this type after the parameter list in
the function heading. The PASCAL system can use this type
information to ensure that the function is subsequently used in an
appropriate context.

Since calling a function produces a single result, we must
indicate, somewhere in the function definition, what this result
is to be. In the function definition the name of the function is
used as if it were the name of a variable to which values can be
assigned. When the function is being obeyed, any value assigned to
the name of the function is returned as the value of the sub-
expression used to call the function.

When the above program is obeyed, evaluation of the sub-
expression "max(a,b)" causes the function definition to be obeyed
with "first" set to the value of "a" and "second" set to the value
of "b". If the function is called when we have the situation

a   4.79                   b   5.64

then the function definition is obeyed with

first   4.79              second   5.64

and the statement

max := second

is obeyed as a result of obeying the if-statement. The value of
the sub-expression "max(a,b)" will therefore be 5.64 and this is
the value which will be used in subsequent evaluation of the
larger expression:

```
max(a,b) + max(p,q) + max(x,y)
```

If the main body of the program had included a statement such as

```
writeln(max(63.45, 61.23))
```

the function would have been obeyed with

first    63.45            second    61.23

and the value returned as the result of the function in this case
would be 63.45, this value being printed by the writeln statement.
The actual parameters can of course be any expressions that will
have real values when the program is obeyed. This means that
the actual parameters in a call of the function can themselves
involve further function calls. We have already seen how we can do
this with the standard functions:

```
z := sqrt(sqr(x) + sqr(y));
writeln(sqr(sqr(sqr(z))))
```

Our function "max" can be used in the same way:

```
writeln(max(sqrt(2), sqrt(3))
```

will print

1.73

and

```
writeln( max(max(6.2, 7.4), max(2.3, 9.5) )
```

will print

9.5

In the last case, the function calls are evaluated as follows:

max( max(6.2, 7.4), max(2.3, 9.5) )
            7.4              9.5
                  9.5

172

Note that in a function definition you should not attempt to use the name of the function anywhere except on the left of an assignment statement. The use of the function name in any other way within the function definition has a special meaning which is beyond the scope of this book.

Functions can also have variable parameters, but the use of this facility is looked upon as being bad programming practice. The reasons for this are rather esoteric and need not concern you.

## 10.6 A final example

In this section we shall write a program which will accept a command to replace every occurrence of a given word in a piece of text with another given word. The input for the program will consist of an edit command on one line followed on the next line by the start of the text to be edited. The edit command could be, for example,

r/daffodil/tulip/

which is to be interpreted as meaning: Replace every occurrence of the word "daffodil" in the subsequent input text by the word "tulip". We shall insist that the edit command is presented with exactly the above layout without the inclusion of any extra spaces. The outline structure we shall adopt for this program is as follows:

```
read the edit command;
if the edit command is incorrectly constructed then
    print an error message
else
    read and edit the text
```

Clearly our program needs to store the two words specified in the edit command in order that words in the subsequent text can be compared with the word to be replaced, and so that the replacement word can be inserted in the output whenever this is necessary. Thus the program requires two arrays of characters into which these two words can be read. In handling these words, we require to know how many characters they contain so that the appropriate number of comparisons can be made, or the appropriate number of characters printed out. We therefore require two integer variables in which to store this information. The character at the start of the edit instruction, and the other three edit command characters will be stored in four other character variables. The text will be handled one word at a time and it is convenient always to read the next word in the input text into another array of characters and to use one more integer variable to indicate the size of this next word. The program therefore requires the following declarations:

```
type word = array [1..20] of char;

var commandletter, commch1, commch2, commch3 : char;
    oldword, newword, nextword : word;
    oldwdlength, newwdlength, nextwdlength : integer;
```

We can now expand our outline program in more detail. The  main
block of the program will be as follows:

```
begin
    read(commandletter, commch1);
    readin(oldword, oldwdlength);
    read(commch2);
    readin(newword, newwdlength);
    readln(commch3);

    if (commandletter <> 'r') or
       (commch1<>'/') or (commch2<>'/') or (commch3<>'/')
    then  writeln('illegal edit command')
    else
    begin
        copypunctuation;
        repeat
            readin(nextword, nextwdlength);
            if same(nextword,oldword,nextwdlength,oldwdlength)
            then writeout(newword,  newwdlength)
            else writeout(nextword, nextwdlength);
            copypunctuation
        until eof(input)
    end
end.
```

Here  we  have  decided to use a procedure "readin" which will read
the next word in the input, store the characters of the word in  a
specified  character  array and insert the number of characters in
the  word  in  a  specified  integer  variable.  This  procedure is
defined as follows:

```
procedure readin(var letter : word;
                 var number : integer);
begin
    number := 0;
    repeat
        number := number + 1;
        read(letter[number])
    until not (input↑ in ['a'..'z'])
end;
```

The   procedure  "writeout"  is  used  to  print  a  word.  It has to be
told  where  to find the characters of the word and how  many  there
are:

```
procedure writeout(var letter : word; number : integer);
var next : integer;
begin
    for next := 1 to number do
        write(letter[next])
end;
```

The other procedure required in the above program is
"copypunctuation":

```
procedure copypunctuation;

var endofpunctuation : boolean;  nextchar : char;

begin
    endofpunctuation := false;
    repeat
        if eof(input) then endofpunctuation := true
        else
            if input↑ in ['a'..'z'] then
                endofpunctuation := true
            else
                if eoln(input) then
                begin
                    writeln; get(input)
                end
                else
                begin
                    read(nextchar); write(nextchar)
                end
    until endofpunctuation
end;
```

A procedure similar to the above was used in Program 9.4 and the
reader is referred to the discussion in Section 9.3.

   In the main block of the program, two words were compared by
using the condition:

   same(nextword, oldword, nextwdlength, oldwdlength)

A condition is written as a boolean expression which, when
evaluated by the computer, has the value "true" or "false". In
this case, the boolean expression takes the form of a boolean
function call. When the computer evaluates the function call, it
will obey the section of program defining the function and bring
back the value "true" or "false" as a result. In this case, the
function definition will specify how to compare the two words
character by character, the value "true" being returned if the
words are the same and "false" otherwise. This function can be
defined as follows:

```
function same(var word1, word2 : word;
              word1length, word2length : integer) : boolean;
var characterno : integer;  stillsame : boolean;

begin
    if word1length <> word2length then same := false
    else
    begin
        stillsame := true; characterno := 0;
        repeat
            characterno := characterno + 1;
            stillsame :=
                    word1[characterno] = word2[characterno]
        until (characterno = word1length) or not stillsame;

        same := stillsame
    end
end;
```

We leave the reader to put together the various parts of the program in the correct order.


Exercises for chapter 10

1) Write a program which draws a rectangle of stars on a background of dots. The size of the rectangle and the size of the background are to be input as data. Your program should use the procedure "writechar" which was defined in Section 10.1.

2) Rewrite Program 9.1 in such a way that the main block starts with the two procedure calls

```
findandread(firstnumber);
findandread(secondnumber)
```

3) A motor rally takes place all on one day and, for each car, a start time and a finish time are recorded. Each car also has a handicap time which is to be subtracted from the true time taken for the rally in order to determine an adjusted time. Write a program which reads the start time, finish time and handicap time for one car and which prints the true time and the adjusted time for that car. Each time is input as two integers (hours and minutes) separated by a space. The program should do all its calculations in minutes, the conversion from hours and minutes being done by a procedure "readtime" which reads a time in hours and minutes; and the conversion back to hours and minutes being done by a procedure "writetime".

4) Write a program to evaluate the expression

$$x^5 + y^4 + z^3$$

where "x", "y" and "z" are supplied as input. Your program should include a function "power" which can be used to raise a real number to an integer power. For example, the expression:

    power(x, 5)

would have the value $x^5$.

5) The measurement of various parts of a fingerprint results in a sequence of ten real values. Two such sets of measurements can be compared by counting the number of corresponding pairs of values which differ by less than 5% of the larger value. Two fingerprints are classified as similar if this comparison results in a count of seven or more. Write a program which reads a set of measurements for one fingerprint found on the scene of a crime and which then compares that fingerprint with the fingerprints of known criminals whose measurements are to be read as further input. For comparing two sets of fingerprint measurements, your program should use a boolean function which can be used as follows:

```
if similar(foundprint, knownprint) then
   .
   .
```

6) The output from a black-and-white television camera is a sequence of pictures, and each picture can be digitized as an array of 400x600 integers, each integer indicating the brightness of one point on the picture.

Write a program which reads digitized pictures taken alternately from two cameras. The first camera is directed at a brightly lit object moving against a very dark background. A point on the background appears in a picture as a brightness value less than 5. The output from the program is to be a sequence of digitized pictures from the second camera with the brightly lit object from the first camera superimposed.

It might be convenient to test your program on smaller pictures, of size 4x6 say.

7) Write a program which counts the number of occurrences of a given word in a piece of text. Your program should use some of the procedures discussed in section 10.6.

8) Write a program which will play a game of noughts and crosses against someone at the keyboard. The person at the keyboard can specify his move by typing the number of the square in which he wants to play. A simple version of the program could make its move by playing in the first empty square it finds. The program should terminate and print an appropriate message as soon as one of the players wins.

# APPENDIX 1

## Reserved words

| | | |
|---|---|---|
| and | function | program |
| array | goto | record |
| begin | if | repeat |
| case | in | set |
| const | label | then |
| div | mod | to |
| do | nil | type |
| downto | not | until |
| else | of | var |
| end | or | while |
| file | packed | with |
| for | procedure | |

**Note:** Some of the reserved words in the above table are used in contexts not described in this book.

# APPENDIX 2

## PASCAL operators

| operator | priority | type of operands | type of result | definition |
|----------|----------|------------------|----------------|------------|
| not | 1 | boolean | boolean | changes true to false and false to true |
| * | 2 | real/int | real/int | multiplication |
| / | 2 | real/int | real | division |
| div | 2 | integer | integer | division with truncation |
| mod | 2 | integer | integer | remainder after div |
| and | 2 | boolean | boolean | logical "and" |
| + | 3 | real/int | real/int | addition |
| - | 3 | real/int | real/int | subtraction |
| or | 3 | boolean | boolean | logical "or" |
| = | 4 | real/int | boolean | equal to |
| <> | 4 | real/int | boolean | not equal to |
| < | 4 | real/int | boolean | less than |
| > | 4 | real/int | boolean | greater than |
| >= | 4 | real/int | boolean | greater than or equal to |
| <= | 4 | real/int | boolean | less than or equal to |
| in | 4 | int/char | set | set membership |

Note: real/int means that the operands can be both real, both integer or any combination of real and integer. Some of the above operators can be used with operands of other types which are not discussed in this book.

# APPENDIX 3

## PASCAL standard functions

| function | type of argument | type of result | definition |
|----------|------------------|----------------|------------|
| abs | integer real | integer real | absolute value |
| sqr | integer real | integer real | square |
| sin | int/real | real | natural sine |
| cos | int/real | real | natural cosine |
| exp | int/real | real | exp(a) is $e^a$ |
| ln | int/real | real | natural log |
| sqrt | int/real | real | square root |
| arctan | int/real | real | arctangent |
| odd | integer | boolean | tests whether an integer is odd or even |
| trunc | real | integer | truncates a real to its integer part |
| round | real | integer | rounds a real to the nearest integer |
| ord | char | integer | converts a character to its ordinal number |
| chr | integer | char | converts an ordinal number into the corresponding character |
| succ | char | char | gives the succeeding character if it exists |
| pred | char | char | gives the preceding character if it exists |
| eoln | file of chars | boolean | tests for end-of-line |
| eof | file | boolean | tests for end-of-file |

<u>Note</u>: In the case of sin and cos the argument must be in radians. The result of arctan is in radians.

# Index